CAN'T LET GO

A JOURNEY FROM THE HEART
OF AFRICA TO AMERICA

RAPHAEL T. TSHIBANGU, M.D.

Copyright © 2021 by Raphael T. Tshibangu, M.D. All rights reserved.

No part of this publication may be reproduced, stored in a retrieval system, stored in a database and/or published in any form or by any means, electronic, mechanical, photocopying, recording or otherwise, without the prior written permission of the author.

Editing and book design: Story Trust Publishing, LLC

RTST Group/Publishing
tshibangu@aol.com

ISBN 978-1-7371350-1-2 (hard cover)
ISBN: 978-1-7371350-2-9 (paperback)
ISBN: 978-1-7371350-0-5 (ebook)

About *Can't Let Go*

Can't Let Go is much more than a tale of rags to riches or the recounting of an immigrant's trials and tribulations. It is not just another rendition of the struggles of belonging—as a newcomer in an unfamiliar land or as a stranger in one's own world where his own people have come to see him as an outsider, nor is it simply about resilience and overcoming. *Can't Let Go* is, in essence, a compelling story of love: a man's love of family and country; a love that is tested, profoundly challenged but still enduring.

This engaging memoir begins in the early 1950s in the quaint little mining town of Jadotville in the Belgian Congo. Against the backdrop of monumental political, economic, and social changes the author, Dr. Raphael Tshibangu, chronicles his improbable journey and spellbinding experiences across continents and oceans, a journey that would take him from his humble, yet proud, beginnings to realizing his adolescent dream of becoming a medical doctor. With vivid details and honest self-reflection, he leads us from his childhood home in a laborer camp to attending some of the most prestigious schools in the United States, thriving and achieving the American Dream as a distinguished specialist in Obstetrics and Gynecology.

As we travel along on Dr. Tshibangu's odyssey, it becomes clear that *Can't Let Go* is also about Grace and Destiny, about the universe unfolding in mysterious and seemingly miraculous ways. In a candid and intimate way, the author brings us with him on his introspective journey and highlights his meandering path from determination and certainty to anguish and ambiguity, and finally to realizations, possibilities and, yes, even enlightenment and happiness.

Can't Let Go is a deeply human story with universal challenges, an inspirational tale that holds a mirror to many among us.

*For my Family, immediate and extended,
near and far, with immeasurable Love.*

Contents

Prologue **9**

Introduction **17**

Homeland **24**

Beginnings **39**

Coming to America **73**

On Family **97**

Enlightened Loyalty **144**

On Gratitude **203**

Epilogue **215**

Appendix **223**

Acknowledgments **239**

Raphael T. Tshibangu, M.D.

Prologue

It was a gorgeous midsummer day, one of the few and cherished balmy days in Rochester, New York—sunny and warm with clear blue skies. The sunrays were gentle and caressing as they bathed the porch of our newly built townhouse in Pittsford, one of the most affluent suburbs of Rochester.

Sitting slightly reclined on a large, coddling purple sofa with my feet on a heavy, rectangular table made of stone and glass, I was calmly, peacefully resting. I had just played a round of golf at Locust Hill Country Club. Shot an 84, which was extremely satisfying.

I was enjoying a cold shandy, or radler, as my kids will call it—my own refreshing mixture of Heineken and ginger ale—while occasionally, involuntarily swaying to a variety of soft jazz and Congolese rumba music that was shuffling on my iPod. It was indeed a wonderful day.

In my reverie, I was asking myself if it could get any better. Could it? Should it? I was calmly and joyfully lost in my American Dream when, suddenly, the harmonious sound of the music was interrupted by the gentle ring of my iPhone. It was a FaceTime call. I picked up the phone and muted the music.

"Hi, Kambo!" There on my phone was the face and voice of my beautiful, smiling, and smirking grandson, Daniel.

"Hi, Danny. How are you?" I said.

"Good," he said, with an amusingly contorted face.

"What are you doing?"

"Nothing."

"Did you have a nice day?"

"Yes."

"What did you do today?"

Just as he was uttering his monosyllabic answer, he was suddenly shoved off the screen as another beautiful, gorgeous, and radiant face appeared. With a slightly rounder face, bright white eyes, bushy, curly and dark brown hair, she was also smiley and mischievous.

"Hi, Elena," I said.

"Hi, Kamboooo," she answered melodiously while emptying her mouth.

"What are you eating, Elena?"

"Strawberries."

"Do you like strawberries?"

"Yes, they are yummy."

That was Danny's three-years-younger sister.

They spent the next few minutes tussling and intermittently hogging the screen. We exchanged pleasantries, talked about food and school and nothings until their patience ran out. It was delightful for me just to watch my grandchildren—without a doubt, the smartest, brightest, and coolest grandchildren in the world.

Afterwards, as they briefly ran off, I finished the call, chitchatting, laughing, and exchanging with my daughter, Titi. Even with the incessant interruptions from Danny and Elena, we managed to catch up on a variety of topics. No shattering news, but overall a pleasant and warm virtual visit. Finally, the phone was silent, the screen went dark.

All was quiet again, but my heart was full. I felt complete.

It was a deep, warm, and blissful feeling. It was a feeling of completeness, which reminded me of another such blissful moment several years prior. It was on the occasion of my sixtieth birthday. My wife, Sherry, managed to organize a truly surprising birthday party. Well, almost birthday, since the celebration was actually on September first, five weeks before my actual birthday.

I was well aware that it was a tradition in my in-law family to host a picnic at the end of the summer. On this particular occasion, my wife informed me that the family had decided to hold a slightly formal and chic affair. Instead of an afternoon in the park, this year's event was planned for the evening and she suggested that we should dress accordingly. I, nonchalantly, chose a pair of trousers appropriate for a fall evening: dark brown with a slight tinge of green. I also picked a long sleeve shirt with a mixture of orange and purple dark stripes that was worn untucked. It was a relatively simple but elegant combination, I thought. Sherry's outfit was svelte black pants topped by a light pink with a tinge of purple, a form-fitting blouse that appeared particularly dressy for such an occasion. Nonetheless, I was quite pleased, as she looked exquisitely beautiful. When we arrived at the venue, I unsuspectingly remarked how calm and quiet the scene appeared. I wondered out loud if we were too early as we approached the front door, but there was no acknowledgment on her part. I had no time to process the surroundings since, just a moment later and with my heart pounding, I was transfixed at the sight of the huge crowd that was quietly hiding behind the large double doors leading to the banquet hall.

"SURPRISE!" they shouted in unison. They were clapping and smiling. The crowd of over 200 spontaneously and beautifully harmonized several versions of "Happy Birthday." All the while, I stood at the entryway in a catatonic state. I was stunned and speechless. As I glanced across the room, I began to recognize the many friends and family that filled the room. They had come from near and far, literally from all over the world. Many were from the vast United States, but they also came from South Africa, the Democratic Republic of Congo (DRC), Liberia, Mali, Canada, and United Kingdom. My mind wandered and wondered: When did they get here? How did they get here? Where are they staying? And when I finally partially recovered from my state of shock from this incredible surprise, all I could feel was the love and the warmth that permeated and enveloped the room. I was truly touched that evening and during my rambling remarks. With all sincerity, I told the gathered crowd that if I were to die at that moment, I would die a happy man. I felt deeply that on my way up to meet my Maker, theirs would be the faces I would love to see. I felt blessed and complete. Just like I felt that beautiful summer day after virtually spending some time with my daughter and grandchildren.

Shortly after that FaceTime call was over, I gradually became more and more conscious of my surroundings. I unmuted the music that was still shuffling on my iPod. I continued to sip my shandy and the music played on.

"Can't Let Go," by South African songwriter and guitarist Jonathan Butler came on and grabbed my attention. From his 1999 album *Story of Life*, the song has a pleasing, smooth melody with a soft, soulful beat. I gradually became more attentive and I replayed the song several times trying to fully digest the lyrics as they clearly spoke to me.

The lyrics touched me, especially since I knew how deeply personal the song was to Jonathan Butler.

Born in 1961 in Athlone, Cape Town, he grew up at the height of the brutal, segregationist, racist, and oppressive regime of Apartheid in South Africa. He was raised in this suburb, more like a shanty town on the outskirts of town, where he was exposed to the hardships of slum life.

It was a life of poverty in a densely populated settlement made of dwellings crudely constructed of tin, mud, wood, or whatever one could salvage; a life of daily struggles with nonexistent infrastructure, sanitation, water supply, rubbish collection, or sewage disposal.

Even while many of the inhabitants of the shantytown—mostly laborers, cleaners, and street vendors—were economically deprived and disenfranchised, they remained resilient and resourceful and maintained a vibrant, traditional culture rich in soul food and music. They not only yearned to escape poverty, but they continued to fight for freedom and independence from this oppressive regime.

Jonathan Butler's musical talent provided him with a way out.

At the tender age of twelve, he won a Sarie (the highest South African music award) and was signed to a major record label shortly after. His career subsequently took off, earning him multiple awards along the way, both in the United Kingdom, where he spent about seventeen years, and the U.S., where he finally settled.

But despite having achieved his dreams of success, freedom and independence, his homeland remained in his soul, calling him and inspiring him in many of his projects.

He could not let go.

So, I listened. And the music played on.

Slowly and uncontrollably, a certain unease came over me and enveloped me.

I was gradually, unwantingly drifting into a mixture of nostalgia, anguish, and melancholy.

I started thinking about the family I left in the DRC; thinking about those that have passed away, many of them prematurely and sadly of preventable causes; those who are still alive, barely, living in abject poverty, miraculously surviving the miserable harsh conditions that the DRC has imposed on them over the past several decades.

Feeling guilt inside?

I was thinking about a recent reference to African countries, including the DRC and many others, as "shitholes." How could a country so scandalously rich in natural resources remain one of the poorest on the planet?

Feeling angry?

I was thinking about the recent anti-immigrant chants of "send them back" or "go back where you came from" uttered by the MAGA (Make America Great Again) red-baseball-cap-wearing zealots; thinking about the overt, blatant, relentless attacks, and expressions of animosity aimed at a group of progressive Democrats nicknamed The Squad, who happened to be nonwhite; thinking about the now freely expressed xenophobic sentiments, racist attitudes, and pronouncements by many under the veil of freedom of speech.

Feeling unwelcome?

I was thinking and drifting further and further into unease. Questions swirling in my head.

And so, what started as a glorious, sunny morning, full of fun and joy, turned into an internally gray and gloomy afternoon full of self doubt, guilt, anger, and many unresolved feelings—and many question marks.

Like Jonathan Butler, I thought I had found the greatest gift of all: the American Dream.

I had crossed so many bridges and inevitably burned so many others. I had played to win and paid the price. But did I do it right? Did I do the right thing? Did I do enough for my family? My country? Am I truly complete?

As I pondered these questions, for what seemed to be an eternity without clear or reassuring answers, I realized that the music was still shuffling and playing on. The iPod had moved on to a more upbeat melody and tempo.

Just like life goes on, changing from season to season, through quiet and turbulent times, I consciously decided to shuffle on and slowly but deliberately started planning the week ahead.

However, from that particular day, I became more and more reflective as I kept retracing in my mind the road I have traveled. I finally decided that I, too, had a story to tell and this would be the time. I say "finally" because, truth be told, for many years, my lovingly tenacious wife had relentlessly urged and encouraged me to document my journey for posterity. "You are the first one here in America; you are the bridge," she would often say. "Who else is going to do it?" And I would usually reply, "What is there to tell?" Occasionally adding there are millions and millions of immigrants with similar stories of fears and anxieties, perseverance and resilience, hope and the endless pursuit of happiness. But now, I also understand that despite the similarities in the stories, mine is unique to me and is indeed worth telling. I also understand that there may not be anything exceptional or extraordinary to tell, but the main reason for my reluctance to write was rooted not only in a certain sense of shyness and humility but also a strong need for privacy. So, it is with my wife's tremendous support and against my shy and introvert nature that I offer in these pages my ambiguous adventure.

Let it be noted that, except for an autobiographical essay I wrote for a college English course in 1971, I have not kept a meticulous diary. Therefore, my story is based on the best of my recollections, often refreshed, corroborated, and/or corrected by extensive exchanges with friends and family during my recent trips to the DRC in 2016 and 2019.

Let it also be noted that my experiences have obviously been shaped by many who have come and written before me. So, whenever possible, I will thankfully acknowledge the source of any specific thought and/or expression. I remain cognizant of the fact that I may inadvertently repeat or rewrite something that has been said or uttered before without according it the deserved credit. While such omissions may be regrettable, I remain grateful and thankful to all.

Raphael T. Tshibangu, M.D.

INTRODUCTION

I**n early November 2019**, I embarked on a pilgrimage that took me to the place of my birth, childhood, and adolescence. A furtive glimpse at the map of the DRC, this vast land mass the size of New England, with its poor, crumbled, or nonexistent infrastructure would reveal how difficult it is to travel from city to city. One needs to have a taste for adventure or be driven by necessity, because such a trip could be an obstacle course with various degrees of challenges.

Nonetheless, it was with some optimism, albeit reserved and cautious, that I planned my journey. Cautiously optimistic, because nine months earlier, Félix Tshisekedi Tshilombo became the first peacefully elected and sworn-in president of the DRC since independence sixty years ago. He had campaigned on restoring law and order, reestablishing peace in the northeastern part of the Congo, and ending corruption. He promised to facilitate and cultivate a favorable climate for investment and economic development. He was determined and full of energy and he had spent his early days feverishly trying to fulfill some of his campaign promises by enacting an ambitious 100-day program. Needless to say, several months into his presidency, many observers would agree that the task would be daunting, as it had always been, but there were signs of progress.

So, with slightly less apprehension than usual, I landed at Ndjili Airport in Kinshasa on November 6. It was a welcoming, comfortably warm, and sunny afternoon. Carrying my American passport, I headed to the Customs and Immigration booth. A few weeks earlier, I was reassured by the consulate office that, as a Congolese American, I could, for the first time ever, obtain my visa right at the airport. Sure enough, as I went through the control, I was relieved and delighted that the formalities were simple, short, and extremely professional.

With my visa in hand, I picked up my bags with none of the usual harassment. What a relief! Within minutes, I walked out of the airport, straight into the inviting, warm embrace of friends Jean Claude and Bena, who were expecting me.

The ride from the airport to downtown, where I would spend the next few days, was long and slow. The highway was jammed with people and cars. The traffic was much slower than usual, crawling in a start-and-stop procession. Even though it took us two hours for a twenty-minute drive under normal conditions, I did not mind because I appreciated the reasons for the interminable traffic jams.

As I quickly learned from Jean Claude Kolamoyi Tshibangu and his wife, Dorcas, roads were being expanded and repaved; new bypasses referred to as *saut de moutons* (overhead bridges) were being built to hopefully reduce the traffic congestions that have plagued this bustling, over-populated city for many years.

I learned and observed over the following several days I spent with Jean Claude as well as my "sister-in-law" (Celestin's wife) Bernadette Ilunga, both entrepreneurs, that the business climate was friendlier, with fewer regulations and less need for corruption. There was a new vibrancy in the air, and I was pleased to witness it.

I thought a lot about my childhood friend Celestin Ilunga, affectionately called Cele, in whom I had strangely placed my hopes and aspirations for the country, but was painfully, prematurely taken from us twenty years earlier. Having chosen a career in the military—in which he excelled and quickly rose to the rank of general by age forty, and serving as a cabinet minister in the last years of Mobutu—he had a pulse on the political and socioeconomic ill-health of the country. Despite the misery we were all witnessing around us, he always gave me hope when we talked about the future of the Congo. His fervent intentions were to *"apporter la prospérité (et le bonheur) à un peuple béni par Dieu"* ("bring prosperity [and happiness] to a people blessed by God"). But he suddenly and tragically died in 2000 at the young age of forty-eight, while vigorously, courageously engaged in his long-term struggle to redress the country's declining path towards worse and worse chaos. He died while serving his country! I pondered about what he would be thinking now, what would he be doing now, if he were still with us.

Several days later, Jean Claude, his wife, and I flew to my next stop, Lubumbashi. This second largest city in the DRC, where I spent many of my teenage years, also showed similar positive changes of burgeoning development. Many of the roads were recently paved and well lit; the downtown area was bustling with activity;

stores and supermarkets were well stocked and a big, famous zoological park near my late brother's house was repopulated and looked beautiful again. I was pleased. I felt hopeful.

Here, I thought a lot about my brother Vincent, who had such a promising executive career at the now defunct Gécamines. I tried to imagine what he could have become, how much more he would have accomplished were he not taken from us prematurely as well. Barely fifty-eight years old, he succumbed to adult-onset diabetes, a sad and tragic example of how even people with reasonable means often died of preventable causes due to the crumbling medical infrastructure. What if...?

A few days later, we drove to Likasi, where I was born. That is where my older brother Zacharie had finally settled in his involuntary retirement. That is also where my eldest and late brother, Alphonse, was recently buried. Paying my respects was the main reason I had decided to travel to the DRC, the main reason I traveled to Likasi. Not much had changed there, except for the wear and tear on the town of the years gone by. Everything in town had stood still except for the ravages of time. Understandably, I became emotionally overwhelmed as I visited the small township and house I grew up in. I was flooded with joyful nostalgia as many happy childhood memories rushed in, and at the same time chagrined at the realization that so little had changed for the better, or more accurately so much had degraded over the past sixty years. Our small red brick house was still standing, a mango tree in front, a flower bush fence, a small clean yard with its uneven reddish clay ground. This place was frozen in time, albeit somewhat beaten up. For a moment, I wished things were different. I wished they were the way I used to imagine and romanticize while listening to Françoise Hardy sing "La maison où j'ai grandi" ("The House Where I Grew Up"), a 1966 song by a young French singer and songwriter whose flourishing career forced her to travel the world. While her friends envied her apparent good fortunes, she could not stop longing for their simple pleasures and happy countryside living; she could not stop longing for the quaint and beautiful house where she grew up. When she left her happy home, she knew she was leaving a piece of her heart. However, she remained hopeful that, one day, she would return to this childhood house surrounded by gardens full of roses and many other flowers. She was hoping to return, one beautiful day, among her friends and their laughter. Alas, things changed.

From Likasi, we then flew to Mbuji-Mayi where my parents were born and are laid to rest. Two of my sisters and most of their immediate families still live there. I thought I was reasonably prepared for what I was about to see, but I could not imagine the shock I experienced as soon as we landed at the airport. This was an unrecognizable, broken down, beaten down city in total disrepair. Half-torn-down buildings with boarded-up windows were everywhere. Many of the hospitals were mostly empty or abandoned despite a desperate need for health care. Roads would turn into rivers every time there was a torrential rain, and motorcycles were the only reliable means of transportation. This was a city were most people miraculously eked out an existence out of thin air. No jobs, no assets, no apparent source of income.

How could it be? How is it possible, I incredulously asked during my entire stay. How did we get here? As difficult as it may have been when my father left this land of his ancestors in search of a better life, things could not possibly have been as bad as this.

So, how did it come to this?

I tried to comfort myself by refocusing on the little progress I had seen days before in Kinshasa and Lubumbashi. And as I flew back to Kinshasa on my way back to America, I was hanging on to the hope that the phoenix could still rise from the ashes.

It had been a long trip and a necessary pilgrimage for me, an overdue reunion. It was a trip full of what-ifs, a combination of introspection and reflections. I was thinking about so many things that had already happened and repeatedly asking what could have been or what could be. I thought a lot about the past and dwelled upon possible mistakes. I thought of unfinished business and tried to figure out if I was to blame. With some regrets and feelings of guilt, I relived many past decisions. And even though, on a rational level, I knew that what-ifs are a curse of human nature and that many people inevitably ask what if, I could not, for a long time, avoid these distressful questions. At the same time, I was noticing that these repetitive thoughts were not bringing me any peace or solace. Instead, they were stealing most of the joy I was experiencing on this trip as I reconnected with my family and a few old friends. I was noticing that with these incessant, wished-for imaginings, I was cheating myself of what was in many aspects a great vacation by focusing on the past and conjuring alternative endings.

So, as I was settling in upon my return to Rochester, I recalled *The Power of Now* by Eckhart Tolle and the lessons learned. I reminded myself that we cannot live in the past while enjoying the present; I reminded myself that, in the end, the what-ifs can only lead to disappointment, melancholy, and depression. "What if frogs had wings?" I recalled a friend of mine saying each time we lamented after a bad golf shot.

But I also reminded myself that these same what-ifs will hurt me only if I let them.

So, I resolved again to put more energy in the present, take action now, do something right now to help amend whatever is hurting me. I resolved to focus more on the things I can control and set more realistic goals. I resolved that, instead of the past I choose the present; instead of fear, control; instead of guilt, absolution, for I am not responsible for the evil in the world but will do as much as I can to help others; instead of lack, gratitude for what I have; instead of complaints about pains and aches, self-care. I resolved to enjoy the story of my life, accepting the past as it was but living to the fullest in the present and knowing that the future I desire is not guaranteed. I finally resolved to start writing My Story.

HOMELAND

THE DEMOCRATIC REPUBLIC OF THE CONGO, previously known as Zaire, the Belgian Congo, and, prior to that, the Congo Free State, is my homeland.

My story is so intricately linked to the vastly unknown, ignored, or sometimes twisted history of this land that a brief chronology is necessary to set the landscape. Many elements are included because of their historical significance, others because of the way they have impacted my life journey.

Although the facts and dates, non-exhaustive as they may be, can easily be confirmed in multiple public sources and the appended publications, any analyses and opinions are mine and mine alone, albeit well informed.

Long before they became confined to the current artificially carved borders, the Congolese people enjoyed an illustrious and prosperous history. It is well documented that the Kongo Empire in the northwestern part of the current DRC thrived for over 500 years from the 14th century. It is also well documented that the Kuba Kingdom Federation in the southeastern part, similarly thrived from 1568 until 1910. They prospered and persevered as sovereign states with good governance well after the initial contact with the West, in

1482, when Portuguese explorers landed at the mouth of the Congo River. They persevered even with the advent of the slave trade in the 1500s. But in the end, internal strife and rivalries, the devastating slave trade, and the envious, devious, greedy grip of Europe proved to be irresistible forces that tore apart these once glorious kingdoms and empires.

The Kuba Kingdom, in particular, put up a fierce resistance against foreign invaders for many years, especially in the 1870s. In the end, however, the resistance movements were outgunned and were no match compared to the strength and brutal determination of King Leopold II of Belgium and his *Force Publique.*

Leopold II prevailed by 1875 and embarked on his Colonial Project, which would become one of the most barbaric, brutal, and exploitative colonial regimes in history. In that age of European rule in Africa, for the sake of exploitation and economic gain, the resources controlled by King Leopold II were being noticed by his European neighbors.

Thus, driven by greed, imperial ambitions, and in search of new economic resources, the leading nations of Europe sought to claim a piece of the African cake for themselves. To that aim, they convened the Berlin Conference from 1884 to 1885. As is widely known today, the conference ended with an artificially divided Africa. Most of the current borders between African countries were established and the major European powers formalized their claims to different parts of the continent. At the end of the conference, with little forethought, King Leopold II was granted the Congo River Basin, with the stroke of a pen. This vast land in the Heart of Africa became a personal property and possession of one man—King Leopold II!

Can't Let Go

Today's map of the DR Congo, centrally located in Africa where most borders were artificially drawn by the Europeans at the end of the 1885 Berlin Conference.

Raphael T. Tshibangu, M.D.

In order to supply Europe with ivory, rubber, and precious minerals, which were in great demand in Europe and highly profitable to him, Leopold II exacted an unimaginable toll on the Congo, slashing its population by as many as ten million in his twenty-three years as an omnipotent ruler, an undisputed God. As recounted by many—including Edmund Dene Morel, the British journalist who launched the Congo Reform Association; Joseph Conrad in *The Heart of Darkness*; Jared Diamond in *Guns, Germs, and Steel*; Adam Hochschild in *King Leopold's Ghost*—under the reign of this monster, no law or restrictions to protect the Congolese people and their land applied. People worked as porters, miners, rubber tappers, wood cutters, and railroad workers. Their bosses and masters were empowered to adopt depraved policies of kidnapping, mutilation, and lynching in order to extract the desired labor and resources from the population. It was not uncommon to amputate the hands and feet of men, women, and children as punishment for not collecting enough rubber or ivory. Leopold's henchmen, called the *Force Publique*, which included many ill-advised Congolese, were the ruthless enforcers who demanded quotas of rubber or ivory from different villages. They violently, severely, barbarically, and devilishly punished the entire village when a quota was missed. Resistance was put down swiftly by killing all those who refused to work and displaying their bodies as a deterrent for others. Sometimes, entire families were killed. Thus, while the death toll can never be truly ascertained due to destroyed records, many historians have estimated that up to 10 million Congolese perished between 1885 and 1908, as a result of killings, maiming, overwork, untreated diseases, starvation, and other factors.

And while most Europeans were profiting and thus remained silent in face of these atrocities, a few in the international human rights movements, such as the Congo Reform Association, campaigned for change in the Congo and ultimately led to the sale of the Free Congo State to Belgium in 1908. This once personal property of Leopold II was taken over by the Belgian government and renamed Belgian Congo.

Regrettably, the brutality, oppression, and exploitation of the Congo and Congolese people did not end with the passing of the reins to the Belgian State. Although not as murderous, the yolk of colonization was strong, palpable, and still reverberates today in the Congolese's daily lives. Notable was the establishment of industrial copper mining in 1911, in the Katanga province, situated in the southern part of the country, and shortly after the establishment of industrial diamond mining in the centrally located Kasai province.

The *Union Minière du Haut Katanga* (UMHK) and *Mines de Bakwanga* (MIBA) would become the largest employers and dominant revenue producers for these provinces, the country as a whole, and more importantly for Belgium. During this period, from 1908 to 1960, a few roads were built and a few railroads laid, only to the extent they facilitated the transport of goods and minerals for export. Schools were built only to the level of secondary education, and trade schools were established only to the extent a reliable, semi-educated labor force was needed. The only two universities in this vast country were not built until the 1950s. The *Universite de Lovanium* in Kinshasa was run by the Catholic Church and the *Universite Officielle du Congo* in Lubumbashi was built by the state shortly after. A few hospitals were similarly built to keep the labor force healthy, given the hard work required of them. And work they did, for a paltry salary and monthly ration of foodstuff in the Company Food Bank.

Compulsory labor or forced labor continued for years without recognition of workers' rights until 1948 when labor strikes, which were started by miners in Elisabethville as early as 1941, but always brutally repressed, became too frequent and disruptive. These strikes finally led to the introduction of minimal wages and nominal improvement of workers' conditions. But these changes were not significant and certainly not enough. So, the 1950s continued to be turbulent years for the Congo, as they were for many other colonies in Africa.

Following the 1959 anti-colonial riots, mostly in the capital city, Leopoldville, the loud cries and calls for Independence were heard in Brussels. Facing the increasing threats of violence, the mounting threat to their economic survival, Belgium strategically acquiesced to the Congolese demands. On June 30, 1960, the Belgian Congo became Congo Leopoldville with its own flag, anthem, and government.

Independent, yes, but in name only. This was yet a maliciously orchestrated transfer of sovereignty, devilishly planned to maintain its dependence on Belgium, thus ensuring the continued pillage of the Congolese resources.

The infrastructure was still rudimentary; the intellectual *cadre* was mostly absent, with fewer than 100 university graduates; the treasury was emptied and a humongous debt was transferred to the new Congolese government. At the same time, the greedy paws of Belgium and its Western allies almost immediately started to foment chaos and division in order to continue their exploitation of the Congo. To that end, secessionist movements launched, in late 1960 in Katanga and Kasai provinces, and were supported entirely by Belgium and their mercenaries, in an attempt to monopolize the rich mining belts of the Congo: divide and conquer. Powerless and inexperienced, the young and fragile Congolese government cried for help to the international community. They were willing to accept assistance no matter where it came from. The United Nations decided to "help" with dubious intentions and a shaky resolve. Shaky and dubious because despite the United Nations' intervention, which was the first and largest to date, consisting of more than 20,000 peacekeepers, the first Prime Minister of the Congo, Émery Patrice Lumumba, was removed from power in a coup d'etat led by a spawn of the *Force Publique,* Chief of Staff of the newly created Congolese Armed Forces, Joseph Désiré Mobutu.

Émery Patrice Lumumba, a patriotic and principled leader, heroically attempted to build a truly sovereign nation. He attempted to steer a neutral course between the West and the Soviet Union at the height of the Cold War. He was willing to accept mutually beneficial assistance wherever it came from. Alas, he was seen as too much of a threat and an impediment in light of the West's own ambitions and plans for this rich country. He was no match for the CIA and the Belgian State Security Service. And unfortunately, in 1961, on January 17, after several failed attempts, the West with the help of local officials including Mobutu finally assassinated Lumumba. They disposed of his body to cover up the crime, cutting it in pieces and dissolving it in sulfuric acid so that there was no trace, no tomb, no martyr monuments. An odious crime for which Belgium would apologize in 2002.

Lumumba had only been in power for less than a year. The West's evil and carefully designed policies of divide and conquer, and of fomenting permanent chaos seemed to be working quite well, as they kept the Congolese people idiotically, blindly busy fighting each other, but just enough to allow for the plundering of the Congo to go on.

Such was the case with the first cleansing of the Baluba people from Katanga province in June 1961, perpetuated by misguided Katangese and orchestrated in Brussels. It was also the case with another Belgian-supported secession attempt of Katanga in 1964. And even more devasting, there was the second CIA-backed coup d'etat by then-Colonel Mobutu in 1965 that would affect the course of the Congo for decades to come.

Unlike his first attempt at exercising authority in 1960, this time Mobutu would not relinquish power. He would consolidate it. He mercilessly cracked down on rivals; he imprisoned many and even hanged some in the public square; he cajoled and intimidated at the same time and managed to build a strong and loyal following using corruption and intimidation. And in 1966, when he nationalized the mining industry, including the UMHK (which became Gécamines), he deliberately and systematically instituted a culture of nepotism, embezzlement, and corruption.

Débrouillez-vous (fend for yourselves) or "Article 15"—as people jokingly would say during those Mobutu years, referring to the then-nonexistent section of the Zairean constitution—was becoming a way of life. People were encouraged to improvise and muddle through as Mobutu was telling civil servants and public officials to "steal moderately, a little cleverly."

In 1971, the Congo was renamed Zaire, as Mobutu embarked upon a campaign of "authenticity." Provinces were renamed, as Katanga became Shaba. Cities with European names were changed to Congolese names. Leopoldville became Kinshasa, Elisabethville became Lubumbashi, and Jadotville became Likasi. Joseph Désiré Mobutu became *Mobutu Sese Seko Kuku Ngbendu wa Za Banga* (the almighty warrior, who, because of his endurance and inflexible will to win, goes from conquest to conquest leaving fire in his wake). Quoting French King Louis XV, he would often proudly say: *"Après moi, le déluge"* ("After me, the flood"). He traded his suit and tie for an abacost and all the officials had to follow suit. He decreed that Christian names were to be abandoned in favor of more authentic names.

But as people scrambled to change their names, the reasons behind this shift eluded most, since all they could see was a slow and gradual decline in their living conditions. As for Mobutu, despite his initial professed intentions to reawaken the national consciousness by emphasizing its own culture and history, the authenticity program soon became nothing but a farce and a façade, yet another tool in the entrenchment of his dictatorship. During his dictatorship, which would last thirty-two years, Mobutu remained on the CIA payroll. He remained America's unquestioned ally in its fight against communism, as Zaire was often used as a springboard against Soviet-backed countries such as Angola. He remained a great enabler for the continued exploiting, plundering, and squandering of the Congolese patrimony. And even after the end of the Cold War in 1991 when Mobutu saw his support from the U.S. dwindle and he found himself forced to open up the country to multiparty democracy, he managed to retain power for several more years.

But times changed, and with each passing day, the West's alliance with this dictator was more embarrassing than useful, and a way out needed to be found. Enter Rwanda.

In April 1994, in less than one hundred days, Rwandan Hutu's so-called extremist government orchestrated a genocide of some 800,000 Tutsis and moderate Hutus. A brutal and bloody civil war engulfed this small country on the eastern border of Zaire. When the Tutsis, led by General Kagame, finally won the war and took control later the same year, over one million Hutus took refuge in poor and disease-infested camps across the border in Zaire. These refugees included, hidden among them, fleeing Hutu soldiers. Two years later, in November 1996, under the pretext of neutralizing the threat of the Hutu soldiers who were supposedly reorganizing and terrorizing the camps, the Rwandan army attacked the refugee camps. Shortly after, under the cover of an anti-Mobutu rebel group, the Alliance of Democratic Forces for the Liberation of Congo-Zaire (AFDL), Rwandans began their march on the Zairean capital, Kinshasa. Tens of thousands of Hutu refugees and ex-soldiers fled westward into Zairean forests, pursued by Rwandan army soldiers, and were brutally and massively massacred.

Given that anti-Mobutu sentiments were so high and support for Mobutu almost nonexistent, there was a yearning for change—any kind of change. So, less than one year after its invasion in eastern Zaire, Rwandan-supported and adeptly led AFDL rebels seized Kinshasa in May 1997, with literally no resistance. In the middle of the night, Mobutu was ushered out of his hideaway in his native village of Gbadolite into exile. He died of prostate cancer five months later and was buried in Morocco.

In the meantime, the head of AFDL, Laurent Désiré Kabila, became president of Zaire. Soon after, he renamed the country the Democratic Republic of Congo, signaling a new and better beginning. However, any hope of peace, reconstruction, and development were quickly dashed. The nationalistic instincts and pronouncements of Kabila, nicknamed Mzee, were clearly counter to the interests of his Rwandan and Ugandan backers who had their own designs for the exploitation of the mineral-rich eastern part of the country.

As Kabila was beginning to purge Tutsis from his government in late August 1998, demanding that they leave the DRC, it became clear that his days were numbered. Using the same prescription, Rwanda and Uganda hastily sponsored and backed an armed Congolese group, the RDC (*Rassemblement pour la Democracy du Congo*), seeking to oust Kabila Mzee. And although their attempt to take Kinshasa in August 1998 failed, repelled by Kabila's own coalition of allies, including forces from Zimbabwe, Namibia, and Angola, the rebel group took and maintained control of large parts of eastern Congo.

The War of the Great Lakes Region was in full force.

Inter-African dialogue, including the Lusaka Agreement of August 1999, failed to halt the fighting. The establishment of a United Nations peacekeeping force in November 1999, which started out with 500 military advisors and would eventually grow to 20,000 peacekeepers over the years, would also turn out to be a colossal failure.

Fighting involving different armies and disparate rebel groups would persist at different levels of intensity until 2020, as the link between the illegal exploitation of the DRC's mineral wealth and the ongoing conflicts became obvious. Calls for balkanization from the likes of French President Nicolas Sarkozy became louder and amplified by stooges in the Tutsi communities in eastern Congo.

There was no longer any doubt that the War of the Great Lakes Region and the push for balkanization were from the beginning, and continue to be, a conflict of access and control of minerals such as gold, coltan, and cobalt—abundant in this region and all extremely profitable, precious, and indispensable for our mobile phones, computers, and electric batteries.

And so it is that under the deafening silence and the glaring self-soothing myopia of the international community, as well as under the lazy, cowardly, possibly enabling eye of The United Nations Organization Stabilization Mission in the Democratic Republic of the Congo (MONUSCO) and the International Rescue Committee (IRC), it was estimated that by 2001, 2.5 million Congolese had perished. And among them the President, L.D. Kabila.

A victim of this international jockeying for control, Kabila was assassinated by his bodyguard in January 2001 and replaced by his hand-picked twenty-nine-year-old son (later revealed to be stepson), Joseph Kabila Kabange, an illiterate, former taxi driver and AFDL rebel. Now the West had found—instead of the more than just slightly but overtly inconvenient Mzee, who was beginning to develop pesky nationalistic tendencies, and through their Rwandan and Ugandan surrogates—yet another puppet who will continue and accelerate the descent of the country, especially the eastern part, into the abyss.

Under Joseph Kabila Kabange, politely called "militia groups" (which were no more than gangs of drugged bandits) multiplied as UN troop numbers grew from less than 1,000 to 6,000 in 2002, 10,000 in 2003, and finally to 20,000 by 2010 where they have remained since. Criminal networks, uniquely established to carry out the exploitation of the country, proliferated nonetheless. By 2003, at least thirty-three international companies were identified as being involved in the plunder of the DRC's mineral wealth while fueling the conflict in the process.

As noted earlier, these gangs—and the companies they protected and enabled—continue to be the cause of the immense suffering endured by millions of Congolese. Rape and mutilations were used as weapons of war, while the lack of medical attention, malnutrition, and famine ravaged those who have been able to survive. By December 2004, the IRC estimated the number of deaths to be about 3.9 million. These grim statistics were also documented in the 2005 Human Rights Watch publication of *The Curse of Gold,* which details the widespread human rights abuses linked to the ruthless efforts by armed groups and multinational companies to control and profit from gold mining in the regions of northeastern Congo such as Ituri, Beni, and Goma. All with no benefit to the Congolese State.

And while this hellish nightmare was going on, the opportunistic politicians were also involved in their power struggles. A bogus election in 2006, boycotted by the main opposition party, Union for Democracy and Social Progress (UDPS), ended predictably with Kabila being sworn in as President of the DRC, in December 2006, for five more years. His main rival then, Jean-Pierre Bemba, would be forced into exile after losing a three-day battle, which my wife and I witnessed up close in Kinshasa. JP Bemba's security guards, carried over from his old militia (gang) had refused to join the Congolese army, and so they, and he, had to go. He lived in exile in Spain until his arrest and imprisonment by the International Criminal Court. He would be finally acquitted and freed in 2018.

This tragic farce would be repeated five years later, in 2011, with the main and eternal opposition leader, Étienne Tshisekedi wa Mulumba, who, despite being widely popular, was sidelined following an election that he had clearly won. He, too, was placed under house arrest shortly after the elections and ultimately banished in exile to Belgium. It was for medical reasons, people were told!

From his exile home in Brussels, Tshisekedi continued his fight for the soul of the DRC until his death on February 1, 2017. Until the very end, he remained a fervent and unyielding nationalist. He was a fighter for democracy and the rule of law. And with his slogan *Le peuple d'abord* (People First), he had unleashed a renewed sense of patriotic service, an increased political consciousness—especially in the diaspora, which became more and more vocal—and demanded the departure, more like ousting, of Kabila.

Kabila, of course, tried, by various machinations, to stay in power, changing the constitution and postponing the 2016 elections for two years. But try as he did, he could no longer stay. The current was too strong this time with incessant calls of *"Kabila degage!"* ("Kabila out!"). Furthermore, and perhaps more significantly, the support from his old masters had evaporated.

So, in December 2018, Félix Antoine Tshisekedi Tshilombo, the son of Étienne Tshisekedi, was elected President of the DRC following contentious and suspenseful elections. He was sworn in in January 2019. It was the first peaceful transition of power in the Congo since Independence.

A ray of hope finally? A light at the end of the tunnel? Or maybe just another rabbit hole. It remains to be seen.

For many years, the Congo has been cursed with so-called leaders who were always puppets empowered by their Western Masters. They have always looked out for their own personal interests and often confused power with true leadership. From King Leopold II to Mobutu and Kabila Kanambe, Congolese people have known and lived a life of hardship and misery, pain, and suffering—untold atrocities, which, for most of the world, are unimaginable and unthinkable. I wonder what Destiny holds for the DRC, my homeland. A place referred to by some as a "shithole." A place known for its indolent plagues, occasionally dormant, occasionally sparing a few, but never ending. A place referred to as a "geologic scandal," blessed with abundant riches and yet still one of the poorest on the planet.

Warts and all, diamonds and all, for good and bad, the DR Congo is my Homeland. My personal story is inextricably linked to its history. I am hopeful that my story can be better appreciated with the backdrop of this much abbreviated, complex, and tortuous account of the DR Congo history.

Raphael T. Tshibangu, M.D.

Beginnings

My father, Raphael Tshibangu Mwadianvita Tshisambu sambu, was born in 1915 in the village of Luamuela, the heart of the Baluba country, on the outskirts of Mbuji-Mayi (formerly Bakwanga). He was of the villages where most of the houses were made of mud and wood and grass; where trees outnumber people; where the air is clean and fresh; where chickens and goats roam freely. He was of the villages where the harvests were sometimes abundant and sometimes meager, depending on the benevolence of mother nature. The catch from nearby rivers and lakes was sometimes rich and sometimes scanty.

I can imagine my father running through the bushes and occasionally hunting for small animals; I can see him swimming and occasionally fishing at the river just like many other boys. Even though a descendant of chiefs, and probably more privileged, he was among the tillers of the soil and fishermen of the rivers, since there were few other employment opportunities or means of subsistence.

For many years, it was all he and his clansmen had known and gotten used to. A relatively simple life, close to nature and even closer to one another with strong traditions binding them together. In this relatively small, simple, and undeveloped place, I know they were happy for the most part.

Until.

Until white men with their white beards started showing up. First with their Bible and Christian names, then with their guns as well as their picks and shovels. Stories about the new cities with vibrant nightlife started circulating. Then, although many fathers were trying to keep their sons with them in their huts, they could only manage to keep them in their hearts, for the lure of the cities and the mirage of booms were too hard to resist.

So, my father left home in 1935 and migrated to Jadotville (Likasi) with his wife in tow. He and my mother, Mukenyi Emerence, were joining many others who had been previously brought in by the Belgians. In the thousands, they were brought in by roads and trains to work in the mines and factories and build good roads, good solid brick houses. My father became employee number 29276 at the *Union Minière du Haut Katanga* (UMHK). To this day 29276 is a number indelibly etched in my mind. It was our lifeline, our social security key. It was his and our passcode to free lodging, cheaper foods at the commissary, free primary schooling, and free medical care.

By all appearances, my father was happy with his decision and his chosen new life. Even though trapped between two cultures, my father amazingly, seemingly comfortably, managed his way in this clearly ambiguous environment. Ambiguous and discordant such that, at his work, he made of whites his shepherds and of himself a sheep who went wherever his white bosses told him, bending his head whenever he approached them often uttering, "*Bonjour, Buana,*" "*Merci, Chef,*" and "*Oui, Chef*" ("Good morning, Boss," "Thank you, Chief," "Yes, Chief") throughout his work day, but outside that province he was his own shepherd, living and conducting himself not as a sheep but as a free, feeling human being, brave and strong minded.

I realize now that I was fortunate that most of my exposure and interactions with my father were seeing him not as a sheep but as a shepherd. Indeed, I always remember a tall, decisive, confident, and caring man. A man full of pride and self-esteem. And in spite of his new Western-oriented society, he was still of his clan. Any sense of vile submission or *étouffement*—of being engulfed by paralyzing impotence in front of the white man and frustrations at navigating the two cultures—was alien to him. He was not like many contemporaries who, having been trained in the European tradition or influenced by it, had their memories and imaginations clogged with the contagion and contradictions of their Western schooling.

My father went to church on Sundays like many others, but he never failed to return to the shrines of his country and to the practice of the best of the Luba traditions. He cared about himself, about his fathers and his ancestors. He seemed to be comfortable in and between the two cultures. He was the past and he was the present. He was both. He was Tshisambusambu Mwadianvita at home and he was Raphael among the whites.

He was also keenly aware about the needs of his many children and the values he wanted to pass on. I remember, among other things, how he would gather us around him after his exhausting workday and would have us repeat in our mother tongue, *Tshiluba*, the magic words, "*Dina dianyi Tshibangu Tshisambusambu Mwadianvita. Ndi muana wa Tshibangu Tshisambusambu Mwadianvita, mukua Kalonji, mukua Mukendi, wa mua Tshibangu Luamuela mu bena Tshitumbila.*" ("My name is Tshibangu Tshisambusambu Mwadianvita. I am the son of Tshibangu Tshisambusambu Mwadianvita, from the tribe of the Bakua Kalonji, the clan of Bakua Mukendi, descendant of Tshibangu Luamuela from the land of Bena Tshitumbila.") These were passwords we had to memorize and be able to repeat at any moment.

Although unclear then, just a bunch of meaningless Tshiluba words, I understood later that my father did not want us to be "nowhere-men." He strongly believed that we should identify ourselves with our honorable forefathers, no matter our station in life and without shame. To a large extent, I now know that I inherited not only my father's full name but I also effortlessly inherited his peace of mind, his ambiguity, his pragmatism, and his tolerance of contradictions with little internal conflict. For instance, I would sincerely tell my teachers at school in my religion class that I did not believe in ghosts and that spirits do not exist, but when I was back home, I was equally accepting of our traditions, as my father would, from time to time, invoke the spirits of our ancestors and even offer a *nzolo ya bakishi* (chicken sacrifice—more like a special chicken dish in honor of our ancestors).

My father would only allow us to speak to him in Tshiluba. He would also and often teach Luba idioms, occasionally tell us frightening stories about ghosts. Sometimes, before we went to bed, he or my mother would recite a *Lusanzu* (an invocation prayer) to their fathers, knowing that, on that enchanted night, they were repeating for their ancestors what, from generation to generation through centuries, the sons of the Baluba had repeated for their forefathers. They did this for us, I am certain, but they also did it for themselves, to reassure themselves that they had not failed in this respect and to prove—demonstrate to all who were listening—that the Luba would not die in them.

Throughout the years they demonstrated, in word and in deed, the many values they wanted to impart on us: hard work and determination, discipline, generosity, responsibility, self-esteem, respect for others, respect for elders.

Like many workers at the UMHK, my father assiduously got up very early in the morning and walked approximately three miles back and forth to his place of work. He, like many others, proudly assumed the responsibility of taking care of their families and the importance of work in that endeavor. In good weather and bad, rain or shine, they walked. They carried their small lunch bag with them and were not to be seen until later that evening. They imparted dedication and determination.

After work, and especially on weekends, he always put on fresh, clean, and well-ironed clothes. He preferred white shirts, which he wore impeccably. He often said, "Be presentable. Be proud."

Mother and Father at Hotel Karavia, 1984. He is sporting an abacost, in conformity with the program of "authenticity."

Always a sharp dresser even when he is just hanging around. Father and Mother, around 1990.

"La maison que j'aimais"—my childhood house; Trabeka, Likasi, 2019.

Mother's visit to the U.S. in 1996. What a treat for her, but mostly for us—my younger brother Albert, Mother, me.

We had to be well groomed. We had to be well behaved so as to bring no shame to the family. He admonished us not to be "*imbeciles*" or "*abrutis*" (jerks). "*Emburti*," as he pronounced the word with a reprimanding rolling "rrr," was one of his favorite expressions when he was displeased with any of us.

Not only was he supportive and encouraging, he was also a gentle disciplinarian. I remember on one occasion we were forbidden from going to play in the nearby Panda River. My brothers and I sneaked out for a few hours, believing that he would not find out, since he was at work most of the day. It is unclear how he discovered our disobedient act, and in his own creative way he wanted to teach us that this was unacceptable behavior. So, once he was settled at his dinner table and ready to eat, he called a family meeting and made us admit our transgression in front of everyone. While forfeiting our dinner for that day, we were asked to stand on one leg and sing repeatedly, "*Musi ende ku Panda, ku Panda, ku Panda—Kulopola samaki, samaki, samaki—Tuli enda ku Panda, ku Panda, ku Panda—Kulopola samaki, samaki, samaki—A tuta enda ku Panda ku, Panda, ku Panda—Kulopola samaki, samaki, samaki.*" ("Don't go to the river Panda, Panda, Panda—Don't go there to fish, fish, fish—But, we went to the river Panda, Panda, Panda—We went there to fish, fish, fish—We promise not to go to Panda, Panda, Panda—We promise not to go there to fish, fish, fish.")

We sang these verses while trying to balance on one leg, without fail so as to avoid additional punishment. We sang while he ate and some of the family members were snickering. We learned our lesson, at least for a while. Because, on another occasion, we were asked not to play hide and seek in the evening because the town was digging some trenches in our neighborhood and it was dangerous to run around, given the extremely poor visibility at night. As usual, we took advantage of my father's absence to join some of the kids in the neighborhood to have a little fun. My father's spy, most likely one of my sisters, informed him of our escapade and here again we were in for an inventive form of punishment. We were asked to carry a large mortar, a common household item, which is a hard, carved wooden trunk with a receptacle on one side allowing for the grinding of maize, manioc, and other foodstuff. One person would hold the mortar while the other put his head in the cavernous receptacle. We would then pretend to play hide and seek. "*Un, deux, trois,… dix. Prêt ou pas.*" ("One, two, three,…ten. Ready or not.") For one person, the mortar was heavy and difficult to carry for a prolonged period of time; for the other, it was difficult to breathe and felt claustrophobic. As usual, we forfeited our dinner, while the rest of the family enjoyed the spectacle. The message was simple, clear, and cleverly delivered.

I must admit that we did not always go hungry following these deserved punishments, because my mother, always caring and nurturing, would sometimes stash away a plate of food that we would later devour while hiding under a bed. She was the ultimate homeostasis manager—supportive of discipline but also verbally or nonverbally providing comfort and affection.

My parents were not only protective, they were mostly generous. They raised many of their nephews and nieces, my father's only brother's children, as their own. Barthelemy Baron Mukeba, Lukalu Elisabeth, Sangana, Masengu—I knew them as my older brothers and sisters rather than my cousins. Despite their meager resources, they were able, willing, and happy to give of their time, money, things, advice, encouragement, and kindness. Even in their retirement years, when they did not have enough or when I sent money and occasionally asked how it was spent, they would often say, "We gave to so-and-so." They gave generously and also reaped generously, as evidenced by the dozens of children and grandchildren named after them. They would always be concerned about others and, from time to time, would tell me, "Do not forget about so-and-so. Do not forget your sisters," he told me just before I left for America.

Brotherhood Bond

I was born in Jadotville in 1952. Now called Likasi, it was a small, clean, pretty, and mostly peaceful city in the Province of Katanga. The Jadotville Hospital was one of the best hospitals in central and southern Africa. Only a pitiful shadow of itself today, it was a large, spread-out complex of one-story, yellow brick buildings with green roofs. Service areas included a maternity wing, surgical wards, internal medicine offices, and many other specialties. It was famous for its quality of care and attracted patients from near and far. It also attracted an occasional malingerer or self-inflicted wound patient in need of a few days of rest and excellent cuisine. It was obviously owned and operated by the mining company UMHK, my father's employer.

The same company, later renamed Gécamines, owned the house that sheltered me for the first ten years of my life. Still standing today, the house was situated in an approximately two-square-mile community or camp called Trabeka in the Township of Panda. This small community was striking in its uniformity, boasting all solid, red brick houses, two to four rooms each, depending on the size of the family. They all had an annexed kitchen, sometimes open and sometimes with a door. They also had a small fenced yard for little-needed privacy since everybody knew everybody else.

Somehow, we managed to comfortably sleep three to four per room. And, although it may be difficult to imagine now, we occasionally could accommodate even more when we had visitors. But as I think about those early years, my recollection is that we had plenty of room to sleep, plenty of room to roam around, and plenty of room to play joyfully.

Most of the roads in Camp Trabeka were either paved or graveled but always well maintained. With little to no traffic and only a few bicycles, the roads also provided additional playground for our football (soccer) matches, rope jumping, tic-tac-toe, or running competitions.

*The last time most of us were all together in one place.
Left to right: me, Zacharie, Alphonse, Vincent; Mbuji-Mayi, 1995.*

Sharing a good laugh during our mother's visit—Albert and me, 1996.

Vincent was the first family member to visit. We tried to show him a good time and took him to Atlantic City, 1982. It was his only visit to the U.S.

*One got out of Dodge for a better opportunity overseas.
My sister Mbombo with her son, Raphael, and daughter, Aimee, 2017.*

With Mbombo; Sweden, 2013.

Life had become extremely difficult in Mbuji-Mayi. Two of my sisters decided to resettle in Kinshasa. Tshika (left) in 2018, Kalubi in 2016.

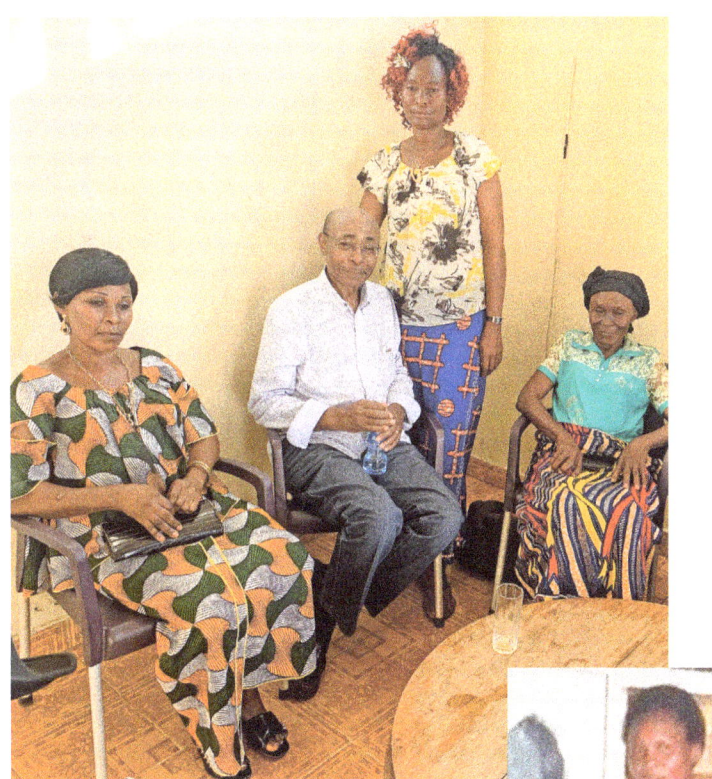

Some are still managing to eke out a living in Mbuji-Mayi. Left to right: Aimee, me, niece Aimee (daughter of Genevieve), Genevieve, 2019.

Right: My sister Genevieve in her heyday, about 1970.

About two to three miles from the house flowed the river Panda, which could easily be accessed through a well-travelled path in the thin brush that surrounded the Camp. This was another source of joyful entertainment, especially for older boys who could swim across the river and tell stories about imagined or embellished adventures experienced on the other side of the bank. One could spend hours fishing, hunting for crickets, or just running around in the bush.

Our toys were homemade; our games and fun activities often improvised. All these activities, which I enjoyed as a young boy allowed my brothers—Alphonse Tshimanga, Vincent Kazadi, Zacharie Mpoyie, and Albert Kalonji—and me to spend a lot of bonding time together.

We were truly a band of brothers. I remember once I got in a fight with some neighborhood boys; somehow, the word quickly reached my bothers. They suddenly appeared and started swinging without a word, without a question. I was happy to see the cavalry come to my rescue and happy to escape without any significant bumps or bruises. It was not until the other boys retreated that they finally wanted to know what had transpired and who was at fault. As it turned out, I started the fight.

They casually admonished me and, hand-in-hand, we walked back home laughing about the incident.

On another occasion, my younger brother, Albert, and I were running around in the playground. He somehow ended up on a nearby street where a passing motorcycle ran over his right extremity. I could not determine the extent of his injury, but it was clear that he could not walk. I instinctively put him on my back and unexplainably carried him to the hospital, about two miles away. Luckily, it turned to be a superficial shin wound and a sprained ankle. When my family asked later how I was able to carry him to the hospital considering his weight, I matter-of-factly said, "He is my brother; he is not heavy."

Unfortunately, those fun days in Trabeka would also be the only time in our lives that we would be all together for any extended period.

First Days of School

I really enjoyed playing all kinds of games with my brothers and really enjoyed making and playing with different homemade toys until I turned six years old. I did not like the idea of going to school. Our primary school, a dozen single rooms in a complex of well-constructed, concrete-and-brick structures, was less than half a mile from home. I was aware of its existence and aware of the purported fun the kids had in school. However, when it was time for me to go, I had no interest and made it clear I did not want to go. Could it have been simple lack of interest or simply fear and anxiety? Most likely the latter. In either case, I remember being accompanied on that first day of school by my fifteen-year-old sister, Genevieve. Incessantly crying all the way to school, my trembling hand in hers, I reluctantly marched on through the school yard and into my classroom where I was forced to remain for the entire session. For the following few days, she continued to walk with me, reassuringly holding my hand and waving goodbye when I was comfortably seated at my bench. Gradually, the back and forth walk to school became shorter and shorter, less and less traumatic. I sometimes wonder if it was not because of the extra-large cookies (biscuits) and warm milk or the sweet and creamy grits (*bouillie*) that were served during breaks that I started looking forward to going to school. In any case, in a few short days my reluctance soon turned into willingness and then eagerness, thus avoiding the dramatic morning scenes that necessitated the comforting hand of my loving sister.

As time passed, I continued to enjoy school, especially since I was doing well at school, and being recognized at home for my success. In his own Pavlovian way, my father would always reward us with a small gift. It was either an extra dessert, a special meal at the table with him, a short trip to visit his friends, or occasionally as an assistant with full access to drinks and snacks during his card-playing sessions with his friends. Always these small gifts would come with calm, warm, and proud words of support and encouragement.

It was often during these private moments that I began to hear a refrain *kasala* (a poetic chant) that he would utter or recite to me many times over the years.

"Tshibangu Tshisambusambu Mwadianvita,
Nzubu kaku hukudi mukua mukodia, muena diyumba.
Lukema Luenda nalu mumpala.
Wa panga nzolu, wa kuata bisonsa.

These verses are packed with meaning, and the following translation is more interpretational than literal.

Tshibangu Tshisambusambu Mwadianvita,
Do not let your house fall apart, the roof fall on your head.

Be protected, blessed, and prosperous.
Keep striving. If you do not catch the chicken at least catch its feathers or the grass around it.

This was his *kasala* for me, his prayer for me, his words of encouragement and empowerment. Deliberately or instinctively, he was praising and motivating me. He wanted me to have self-esteem, self-confidence, and determination. He wanted me to pursue my goals and prayed for me to succeed in my endeavors. And, even though I did not appreciate their full meaning initially, these few Tshiluba words, ingrained in my memory since, have remained as powerful and relevant today as they were then.

True to those words, playtime became secondary and my studies a priority. I worked hard and performed well in school, often being first or second in all of my classes. I was being noticed by teachers and students for this performance; so much so that by my fifth or sixth grade, I was being accused of witchcraft, since no one could be so smart as to always be first or second!

This kind of accusation or thinking was not unusual or uncommon then, and it is sadly still prevalent today. In many parts of the Congo, reason or rational thinking often goes lacking, giving way to the supernatural and metaphysical. Nobody succeeds by virtue of talent, intelligence, or hard work alone; they must be into witchcraft or mysticism. Similarly, nobody dies of natural causes; they must be victims of mischief, sorcery and/or witchcraft. Even educated and/or religious individuals often diminish others' accomplishments by attributing them to the occult so that they can self-forgivingly justify their own failures and thus readily embrace victimization.

Unfortunately, it is also why celebration of one's accomplishment is often muted by the celebrant and often replaced by envy and jealousy or, at worst, ill wishes, intentions, sabotage, or even physical elimination by those who did not succeed. Sadly, even today, it is jokingly said that poisoning is a favorite Congolese sport. Somewhat true, but sad and pathetic.

These widespread beliefs did not then—and still do not—influence my day-to-day actions. I never let talk of sorcery bother me, and, in fact, I often laughed at such utterances and laughed when someone pretending to be joking would ask me to pass on some of my wizardry or *lawa ya hakiri* (medication for intelligence).

As the saying goes, *"Le coeur a ses raisons que la raison ignore."* ("The heart has its reasons that reason does not know.") So it can be said that "traditions have their reasons that reason does not know." With that in mind, I acknowledged many of the traditions but did not allow them as much as possible to interfere with my rational thinking.

I did not allow them to interfere with my Christian upbringing either. Like most Congolese in this area of the country, I grew up as a Catholic. I was a devoted Catholic, an enthusiastic choir boy, an angelic acolyte. I was so devoted that on my First Communion day I was secretly wishing I would die so that I could go straight to heaven. I believed deeply that, at that specific moment, I was the purest, the saintliest that I could be. Needless to say, that wish was never granted. I remained, however, a good Catholic and a good student.

The UMHK had a mandatory retirement age of fifty-five. A small token of a pension to barely cover expenses such as housing, food, clothing, usually accompanied this forced departure. In true capitalistic fashion, relatively healthy, strong, and vigorous men were being replaced by younger, stronger, and cheaper workers, leaving many heads of household to descend deeper into poverty, fending for themselves and still needing to do odds-and-ends jobs to supplement their meager pensions.

So, in 1963, shortly after his involuntary termination, my father was suddenly unemployed. The inevitable "what next" must have consumed him, considering his still significant family obligations and responsibilities. With dimmed prospects of finding another job given the prevalent social and political climate, he decided to return to his native village of Luamuela, where the cost of living would be much more affordable.

I am sure the fact that barely a year before, ethnic conflicts between the Katangese people and the Baluba from Kasai, which pushed us in a refugee camp for several weeks, was also a motivation for him to go back among his people. Rather than stay in Likasi where the future was uncertain and where he was an intermittently unwelcome small fish, he preferred to go back home. He would take back his place next to the tribal chief. He would truly become a big fish in a small pond.

Thus, literally overnight, I was separated from my family.

My four sisters, Kamwanya Genevieve, Kalubi Clementine, Tshika Marie, Mbombo Souzanne, and my two younger brothers, Albert Kalonji and Benjamin Tshiunza, were on their way to Kasai. They would join Barthelemy Mukeba, Sangana, and Masengu who were already there. Lukalu remained in Kolwezi where she was well established with her growing family. My three older brothers, Alphonse Tshimanga, Vincent Kazadi, Zacharie Mpoyie, and I were left behind, scattered in different locations, to pursue our education.

Our parents must have determined, and the boys agreed, that they were full of promise and they would carry on. They would make our father and our family proud.

They were all suddenly thrown into adulthood.

The oldest, Alphonse Tshimanga, was finishing his training in *outillage* (tool and die) at a local trade school. He successfully completed his training a year later and immediately started working at the same company where my father worked. Either because of loyalty, which was a common trait back then, or, most likely, for lack of options, he would work for the same company as my father did until his mandatory retirement thirty-five years later. He would witness firsthand, the brutal transition of the UMHK to the nationalized Gécamines; he would witness and endure the slow, cruel, devastating fall and bankruptcy of this once powerful and promising engine of development and subsistence to many.

The second older brother, Vincent Kazadi, was a junior in high school when our parents returned to Kasai. He was attending College Ruwe, a reputable preparatory boarding school run by Jesuit priests and tucked away in the small rustic village of Ruwe, about halfway between Likasi and Kolwezi. He subsequently attended the prestigious Lovanium University in Kinshasa, which was then one of the best institutions of higher learning in Africa. About six years later, at the Lubumbashi campus of the university, he finished his training and became one of the first handful of metallurgical engineers in the country. He too worked at the UMHK. He quickly rose through the ranks while enjoying the better perks, which were, at the time, only reserved to white executives.

He lived in an exclusive community with fenced-in, large, luxurious houses that were manicured by private gardeners and protected by impeccably dressed sentinels. He had access to the company-sponsored country club where my nephews learned to swim and enjoyed ice cream cones on hot days. He not only had access to a company car, he was also driven by a private chauffeur for his business and personal affairs. He had a maid, a cook, and a house cleaner. He had all the trappings of success, albeit for a short while. He was light-years away from the life we had known just a few years earlier in Trabeka and far away from the River Panda. But, he too would witness the dramatic fall of Gécamines and would endure its consequences.

The third older brother, Zacharie Mpoyi Kasonga, was also at a boarding school, which he successfully completed before attending a technical institute in Likasi. He became an electronic technician/engineer. Breaking with tradition, he chose to work for the main railroad company, *Société Nationale des Chemins de fer du Congo* (SNCC), where he would also, in short order, join the ranks of directors and executives. He quickly became a *cadre*. And for many years, he enjoyed some of the perks that were there too reserved for white expatriates and executives. He and his family would spend most of their glorious years in Kolwezi until the Baluba ethnic cleansing in 1992 forced them to abruptly relocate to Mbuji-Mayi, leaving most of their assets behind. A spiraling, dramatic fall from riches to rags would follow for lack of steady and meaningful employment.

Clearly, at least for a while, it appeared that our father's decision to leave them behind to pursue their education was unquestionably the right one.

As for me, the decision was not as clear cut. To go or not to go? I was given an option in this momentous decision. I was enjoying my primary school and was doing well. I was finishing fifth grade then and I knew how important education was to my parents. Their preference was for me to stay, but they would gladly take me with them if I so wished.

I chose to stay.

I cried a little each day as I gradually and fully realized that, for the first time ever, I would be completely separated from all my immediate family members, for an unknown, but seemingly endless, duration.

Once the decision was made, however, my father tried to reassure me that it was for the best, that primary school will be over soon and I will be one of the big boys. He promised he would visit often and arranged for me to stay with a very close family friend, Kalonji Emmanuel, who had graciously, generously, lovingly accepted the added charge to his already large family. Being retired and unemployed, my parents did not have the means and did not visit as often as promised.

Nonetheless, I was well taken care of by my new guardians, my new extended family. I was learning to live without my immediate family members for prolonged periods of time.

And thanks to the warm embrace and support of my guardians, my school performance did not suffer at all, as I continued to perform at the top of my class. I must have caught the attention of the school administrators and counselors who, behind the scenes, enthusiastically secured my admission to Collège St. Grégoire, another Catholic boarding school in a small village of Karavia on the outskirts of Elisabethville (Lubumbashi). I would soon discover that St. Grégoire was one of the best schools in the country and that I would soon count among its small but select student body.

The Universe was unfolding.

A few weeks prior to moving from Likasi to Lubumbashi, my brother Alphonse, who had just started working and had the benefit of his company housing, had remodeled his kitchen by installing an aluminum door to enclose and secure it and also furnishing it with a bunk bed as well as a small table. He wanted to show me that I would have a place to stay when I returned from the boarding school. He wanted to show me that even though moving to Lubumbashi meant moving further away from the rest of the family, even though it meant adjusting to a new environment and meeting new people, he had my back and I could always count on him. He did so in his calm, quiet, gentle, and protective way. And indeed, at that very moment, I felt comforted and protected.

From that moment on, I felt safe and secure. And, on the day I left for school, I can still remember his warm hand enveloping mine as we walked mostly silently to the train station. He was again telling me without uttering a word that we were a family; we had each other, no matter the distance separating us.

Until his untimely death, in March 2019, following an accidental hit by a motorcycle, this diminutive man remained a gentle giant, a good and caring man, a protector. He remained the family peacekeeper, a respectable and widely respected brother, father, and grandfather.

Karavia

The train station was bustling with activity, a mixed and seemingly orchestrated cacophony. There were incessant loud and sometimes screeching noises of arriving and departing trains; there were busy small vendors hustling and selling anything from souvenirs and artifacts to fried fish, bread, bananas, manioc, and peanuts; there were also busy families kissing and hugging and saying good-byes.

On that particular day, I observed at least a dozen kids my age, nervously and tightly clutching their small suitcases or bags. Strangely, the look of fear and anxiety on many of these young kids helped dissipate my own lingering anxieties, still present despite my older brother's reassurances. I was not alone on this journey.

Our boarding was announced. Time for a last hug, a short walk alone, a furtive look behind, and I was finally on the train heading to my new destination: Karavia, Lubumbashi. I had been on train rides before with my brothers, but I still remember vividly the fear and excitement of this first train ride to Karavia. Unlike the previous times when we traveled packed like cattle in an economy car to and from Kolwezi or Mbuji-Mayi, this time we had our own reserved car with free food and drinks. There were several upperclassmen who acted as chaperons and quickly reassured most of us. We snacked on cookies and *tartines* (slices of bread) and drank Coca-Cola and Fanta (orangeade). This made the two- to three-hour trip more fun and even enjoyable as we traveled to this yet unknown destination.

And over the subsequent years, I would immensely enjoy these rides and would often look forward to them with gleeful anticipation. On the way to school, I was looking forward to reuniting with my new friends, exchanging stories, and sharing snacks as well as an occasional cigarette. The train was like a free zone with little-to-no supervision, allowing us to run around between our two cars as if we were on a playground. On the way back, I was looking forward to the fun on the train, a much-needed break, a respite from the tedious, rigorous school schedule.

The official name of the boarding school was Collège St. Grégoire le Grand, but we affectionately called it Karavia and proudly referred to ourselves as Karaviens. Built and run by Benedictine priests, it was situated about five miles from the center of town in the small village of Karavia. It was surrounded mostly by a lush brush interrupted by small one- to three-room dwellings, which housed many of the workers who maintained the school and performed other essential jobs such as cleaning, cooking, and gardening.

With an all-male student body of about 200 boys ranging from eleven to nineteen years of age, Karavia was one of the best secondary high schools in the country. We had a reason to be proud Karaviens, as we soon learned that this small place had already contributed significantly to the still anemic but burgeoning *cadre* of the Congo. Karaviens were well represented in all the professions including law, medicine, engineering, as well as politics and the arts.

For many of us, this would be the place where we would prepare ourselves to enter these professions. It was where we developed lifelong friendships and forged new families. It was here that we became adolescents and then men, in quick succession.

We lived together, twenty-four hours a day most days. Every hour was planned and choreographed. Wake up at 5:30 a.m. to the sound of classical music, such as Beethoven, Mozart, or Handel.

Class of 1970—Marcel Kazadi and me in front; Cele is standing far left.

We entertained ourselves in many ways and occasionally staged plays. This is the cast of Maitre apres Dieu *by Jan de Hartog. I am standing 4th from left, 12th: Banza Nestor, 13th: Tshiany, 15th: Nyembo Oderic.*

A mini reunion in Pretoria, South Africa, where Cele had moved his family. Left to right: Tshiany, Cele, me, 1998.

Many of us were doing relatively well despite the worsening conditions in the country. Cele (left) and Marcel; Kinshasa, 1995.

Following a stint as a math professor in Gabon, my old friend, Ilunga Mbuyi (Yayop), settled in Canada after spending some time with us in Rochester. He is accompanying me at a dowry ceremony for my nephew Douglas, 2003.

Then, make up the bed, pick uniform and iron if necessary, exercise, shower, and get dressed, morning prayer in the Chapel prior to breakfast at 7:00 a.m., classes from 8:00 a.m. to noon with only ten minutes between classes, lunch together, brief afternoon classes followed by sporting activities or property maintenance chores on alternate days, another shower and another change of uniform before evening prayer in the chapel, dinner followed by a study period, and bed by 9:00 p.m.

For the younger students (First and Second Orientation Cycle), the sleeping quarters consisted of a large, open room with dozens of beds, while the older students, upperclassmen, had their own much cozier rooms accommodating eight to ten per room.

The discipline was strict and militaristic and could only be appreciated in retrospect. Under the threat of punishment, which often consisted of more chores: beds had to be made precisely as instructed, our meager belongings neatly arranged, our khaki uniforms clean and sharply ironed.

Beyond the inevitable adolescent complaints about too many rules, occasional complaints about bad food, sporadic rebellious moaning and groaning about the rigorous school schedule and the value of learning Latin or Greek, most of us retrospectively realized that Karavia was a great school and we were privileged to count among its graduates. Karavia was more than a school, a place of teaching and learning, it was a nurturing place. It was a family away from family, a training ground that raised a band of brothers. It was a place where those of us who made it through got our saving grace. It was a place where we held each other's hand, confidently walking towards manhood.

Raphael T. Tshibangu, M.D.

As it often happens under these circumstances, tight-knit groups were formed with even stronger and forever bonds of friendship. Not to be an exception, I belonged to such a group. Our small group of five often sat together in the dining hall; we studied together, played checkers or Ping-Pong together, and together we danced, when permitted on a Saturday night, to the music of Franco Luambo, James Brown, or Johnny Hallyday.

I remember fondly my dear friend, the late Marcel Kazadi (Morceau), who on a few occasions gave us a taste of the good life when he invited us to visit his sister who was already a *cadre* at *Gécamines* with full privileges of its country club. We looked forward to *frites* (french fries) and tomato with mayonnaise sandwiches among other delicacies that we could not get at school or at home.

By far the most athletic and the best football player of the gang, Morceau was also a great writer. But instead of a future in the sports or the arts, he became an engineer and a geologist. We remained close since our early days at Karavia, and I was fortunate enough to visit him multiple times in Kinshasa over the decades and to host him a few times in Rochester during his visits to the U.S.

I also remember with a smile, the deceitfully quiet and extremely funny Mbuyi Crispin. He was the joker who delighted us with his interesting interpretations of bible stories such as Sodom and Gomorrah or the many wives of Abraham, which he read more for entertainment than for spiritual inspiration or growth. A few others such as Banza Nestor, Tshikunga Philippe, the late Tshiany Tharcisse, Pediatrician; Kabeya Charles (Kachaff), Urologist in Zimbabwe; Katumba Baudoin, Neurosurgeon in South Africa; and the late Mbuyi Ilunga, Professor in Canada, were permanent members of our Karavien family.

During vacations, as we each returned to our respective homes, some of us remained very close. Such was the case with my best friend Celestin Ilunga a.k.a. Shamanga. Cele, as we called him then, lived in the same town of Likasi but in a different section of town. This section, called Cite Kikula, was about four miles away from Panda, where my older brother lived.

Even though it was a long one-and-a-half to two-hour walk each way, it never appeared to us to be that long a distance. Even when I would walk from the Workers Camp in Panda and weaved my way through the Executives Section, Macomeno, with its fancy big houses owned by the white expatriates and few black *cadre*, even as I walked by the clubhouse—which I told myself I would be able to frequent soon—it did not seem that far; even when I was dodging loud motorcycles and cars, which I told myself I would be driving soon, it did not seem that far; even while I was sweating under the scorching, suffocating, and unbearable sun, it did not seem that far. Rain or shine, we would see each other at least once during short breaks, which I spent mostly in Likasi. Ours was a loving friendship, an enduring friendship, a brotherly friendship.

It was also a competitive relationship, which often resulted in anxious anticipation at the end of each trimester as we wondered who would be first and who would be second in our classes. We often alternated those two positions in our class standings. And fortunately, whoever was the winner would usually celebrate quietly and respectfully. We were happy for each other's achievements and we knew that, no matter what, we would always be there for each other.

Karavia's curriculum was of a liberal orientation. After the first two years, each student would choose to concentrate either in *Section Littéraire* (humanities) or *Section Scientifique* (sciences). I chose the sciences. I enjoyed and excelled in mathematics, physics, and chemistry. At the same time, we read extensively (and obviously) mostly French authors such as Moliére, Malherbe, Stendhal, Sartre, Camus, and many others. One of those books, *La Peste* (*The Plague*), would have a lasting influence on my life and career choice.

Written by Albert Camus in 1949, *The Plague* is a fictional tale about a small coastal town in Algeria, called Oran. The inhabitants in Oran were simple and ordinary people. Sometimes happy and sometimes sad, the people of Oran were merely going about their ways, taking things for granted, often ignorant or unthinking about the complexities of life and death. They were like many other people and many such small towns. However, when rats started dying in large numbers in the streets and people followed suit, the Plague was finally diagnosed as the culprit and the town needed to be quarantined.

As he developed his main characters in the book, including the priest, the mayor, the doctor, the journalist, and sanitation workers, Camus paints a gripping tale of human disease, horror, fear, and despair. He tells a tale of survival and resilience and the way in which humankind confronts life and death. He vividly portrays the way we confront unimaginable extremes of suffering, which brings out the worst in some and the best in others. It is thus a tale of me and we, a tale of egotism and selfishness, as well as compassion and selfless heroism.

This story profoundly resonated with me, especially in light of the realities and sufferings that I was gradually becoming aware of in my country. Rieux, the doctor and the narrator of the book, was my favorite character, my biggest influence, and I later subconsciously adopted him as my role model.

I knew then, at age sixteen, that I would become a doctor.

And even though I had previously dreamt of becoming an engineer and a *cadre* in the mining company, as I longed for their lifestyle of luxury—even though for unknown reasons I thought about becoming a pilot, which I still occasionally do in my sleep dreams—there was no doubt in my mind that I wanted to be, that I would be, a doctor one day. I obviously had no idea at the time what path I would follow or what would be required to achieve my goal. But I did not worry about details then. I did not waste time asking the hows, I knew the whys.

Raphael T. Tshibangu, M.D.

Coming to America

Shaken but Not Deterred

During the last two years at Karavia, we often frequented the American Cultural Center, located in the American Consulate. It was located in the center of town, about an hour-and-a-half to two-hour walk from school. We always looked forward to this enjoyable excursion. Taking advantage of the rare free time from our busy schedules, we would gladly, excitedly, take the trip downtown. We would people watch, window shop, and occasionally treat ourselves to a refreshing ice cream when we could afford one. We then stopped at the Cultural Center where we would read—more like look at—*Time* and *Newsweek* magazines, as well as other newspapers and magazines that gave us a glimpse of American life.

Many of my classmates were interested in pursuing their studies in Europe, Belgium, and France in particular. I was quite hesitant, however. I had learned that some French schools were offering medical degrees that were good for practice only in Africa. I would later find out that this was only partially true. Nonetheless, at the time,

I did not want to be told where I could and could not practice. Not only would this be too restrictive but it also struck me as discriminatory and insulting. Therefore, my eyes were set on the United States instead. And, it was through the American Cultural Center, that I heard of the Africa-America Institute, commonly known as AAI.

Founded in 1953, AAI is a U.S.-based international organization dedicated to increasing educational opportunities for young Africans and improving global understanding of Africa. Although it presently focuses on postgraduate studies and training, for a few years in the late 1960s part of the program was designed to assist undergraduate students as well. So, with the help of my school counselors, I applied through AAI to the usual well-known and prestigious schools, such as Harvard, Princeton, Stanford, and Berkeley. I felt that I was qualified and therefore did not have a plan B, nor do I recall having any particular concerns as I waited for a response.

The reply was unexpected and somewhat surprising. In brief, it read close to the following, "We regret to inform you that you were not accepted into any of your chosen schools." However, it went on, "We have secured an admission for you at Amherst College if you choose to accept it."

Amherst?

Confusion and disappointment. I had never heard of Amherst College. I knew that not all colleges were good and reputable. I certainly did not want to attend any no-name school and be limited or restricted in my pursuits, I kept telling myself. In that case, I could just as well go to France, I thought, despite my initial misgivings. I could even attend the local university and forgo my dreams of an overseas education.

A decision was awaited from me and I did not have the luxury of time.

Destiny would have it that on one of our afternoon excursions to the Cultural Center, a chance encounter with the American Consul would rescue me from my predicament.

"And you, where are you planning to go to school?" he said to me in French.

"I do not know," I replied. "I wanted to go to the U.S. but was not accepted in any of the schools I wanted. But I have an offer from Amherst College," I added with a disappointed tone.

"Amherst College?" he asked incredulously.

"Yes. But I am not sure… I do not know."

"You have to go. You really have to go. It is an excellent school, one of the best. I know it very well."

He knew it very well indeed. He was a graduate of Williams College, a close relative of Amherst, as I would soon discover.

My decision was serendipitously being made on the spot. I told myself—*convinced* myself—that if this American high diplomat could enthusiastically recommend this school, I absolutely had to go.

Alea iacta est. (The die is cast.)

I did not wait for my high school graduation ceremony, nor did I care for the results of the university-required *Examen d'état* (state exam). I was going to America.

So it was, in late June 1970, that with excited anticipation I boarded a Sabena airlines flight from Ndjli Airport to Brussels. After approximately eight hours of a rather enjoyable flight, we landed in Brussels in the middle of the night, greeted by a bright sky with millions of flickering and welcoming lights. Since my next flight was not scheduled until the next morning, I, with other transit passengers, was taken to George V Hotel for the night. It was a deluxe, grand, five-star hotel that exuded more luxury and opulence than I had ever seen. My impression of overseas was so far exhilarating. After a restful night and a free breakfast provided by the hotel, I was ready for the next leg of my voyage. I was still very excited and glad to be finally flying to America.

However, very soon and almost abruptly, excitement turned into dread and panic. It was as if a switch was turned on as soon as I reached my seat and buckled my seat belt. Nothing in my previous experiences, some of which were quite adventurous, compared to this first transatlantic flight.

It was a large, cavernous plane populated by mostly white passengers. It was busy and noisy. As I wiggled my way into my assigned middle seat, the space suddenly appeared much smaller than it actually was. My fellow passengers on each side of me seemed nice and courteous. I could tell by their smiles and their body adjustments in their respective seats as they tried to accommodate my presence. They must have said something to me since they were looking at me and appeared to be speaking. But I did not understand what they were saying! Could not make out a single word! Am I on a wrong plane? I cannot remember whether I spoke or even attempted a smile. I do not remember much about the flight except for the hum of the plane and the "strange" language being spoken around me. I do not remember much except for feeling squeezed in my middle seat, feeling suffocated, and wishing I were back home. Whatever fears and anxieties I had experienced as a child on my first day of primary school, whatever fears and anxieties I had experienced as a fifth grader when my parents left me in Likasi, nothing in my memory could compare to this. This was a full-blown panic attack, as I would later understand it to be.

During the last two years of high school, many of my classmates and I thought that we could speak English semi-fluently. We felt confident that we could read and write English, even though it took us several class sessions to get through a single issue of *Time* or *Newsweek*. We were also listening to music from British performers such as The Beatles and American performers such as James Brown and Otis Redding. We certainly could sing along even though we were not always sure what the lyrics meant. Furthermore, on occasions we would proudly show off our fluency and proficiency by exchanging a "Good morning," "How are you?," "My name is...." This knowledge gave me some level of confidence as I embarked on my adventure to America. Others with less preparation have made it. Surely, I would do just fine, I had told myself.

So, when I boarded the plane and realized, shockingly, that I could not understand a word when people around me where speaking American English, my mind could not bear the thought of not being able to make it. What if I am sent home because I could not speak or understand English? I must have asked myself "what if" a million times during those few seconds. My mind could not fathom the possibility of failure. And yet, there I was, all alone, with a one-way ticket to New York. There was no way back. And even if I could go back, could you imagine how devastating it would be for my family, how mortally embarrassing it would be for me to face my family and my true friends who were expecting so much of me? How could

I attend university if I do not understand or speak English? Am I going to make it? What if I do not make it? What would I do? What would my family say? What would my friends say?

What if... What if... And this went on for seemingly an eternity.

I remained anxious and mostly absent during and throughout this horrible transatlantic flight.

I do not remember landing at JFK Airport. My short stay in New York City, where I met with my AAI sponsors, remains mostly a blur. I also do not remember exactly how I traveled from New York to Washington, D.C., where my amazing sponsors had already enrolled me in the intensive English-language program at Georgetown University.

On the contrary, my memories of Georgetown remain vivid and mostly pleasant, as I thankfully and quickly recovered and refocused on the purpose of my journey.

My apartment near Dupont Circle was a short bus ride to the university in a modestly maintained brick building with a mostly grey painted façade. The apartment building was home to many francophone students from Ivory Coast, Algeria, Senegal, and Togo who were also attending Georgetown. I shared my apartment with a student from Tunisia and I was happy about the selection my sponsors had made for me. Reassuringly, we both immediately realized that many of us were in the same boat. With minor differences in our fluency, we were all barely speaking and understanding English. Most of us had just finished secondary school and were hoping to start advanced studies at different universities in the fall. That early realization allowed me to breathe easier and convince myself that if any of them could make it, then I certainly could.

I became more present. I began to relax and began to enjoy my American journey.

I was also fortunate that shortly after my arrival, the Congolese Embassy had a celebration for Independence Day, June 30. It was, from my then-limited perspective, a large and pompous event held at the Mayflower Hotel in Washington. It was a formal and elegant affair, the likes of which I had never attended before. So, with a borrowed jacket from my apartment mate and a fancy invitation obtained through AAI, I found my way to the luxurious Mayflower. I met and joyously mingled with many of my countrymen. And even though we were meeting for the first time, as often happens with strangers in a strange land, we behaved as if we had known each other for a very long time. Those who had been in the U.S. for a while were extremely cordial and welcoming. They eagerly offered their assistance and shared a few survival tips. All were encouraging and were trying to instill a sense of confidence in me. If you successfully finished secondary school in the Congo, they would say, you will certainly do fine. They would remind me that I chose to be here and belonged here; that mastering the language was only a short-term challenge and, in the long run, there is power in being multilingual. Indeed, later I would understand that, as people were often impressed that I spoke so many languages. And the advantages would become even more obvious when much later we started travelling around the world.

They also advised me to shed my social anxieties and try to network with other African or Congolese immigrants so that I could create a safe place where I could de-stress, unwind, and be myself. Not only would networking help alleviate the inevitable feelings of isolation and loneliness, it would help in staying connected and may even open up unforeseen opportunities. They suggested I buy a few Congolese music albums with artists such as Franco Luambo, Docteur Nico, Tabu Ley Rochereau, and Pépé Kallé to soothe those moments of nostalgia or homesickness. Some even offered to send me some African foodstuffs from time to time if I wished. Finally, a truly enjoyable experience in America.

We promised to stay in touch after the reception, and, fortunately for me, some of my new aquaintances reached out to me shortly after. They took me out so that I could finally appreciate the grandeur of the Capital City and its famous tourist sites. We visited the White House, Lincoln Memorial, Washington Monument, and so on. They also opened up their homes. They provided me with an oasis where I could speak French/Swahili and converse without straining, where I could comfortably listen to Congolese music and eat home-cooked Congolese delicacies. Without hesitation, I can truly say that I enjoyed my time and Georgetown. I remain grateful to my teachers at the English Institute and grateful to the Congolese community whose support allowed me to refocus on the task at hand.

Alas, time did not stand still. Eight weeks of intensive English zoomed by. Throughout, the fast-running calendar was reminding me that in a few short weeks I would become a college student.

Amherst

Nestled in a picturesque western Massachusetts small town of fewer than 30,000 people, Amherst College is one of the "Little Ivy League" schools often ranked among the Top 20 Best Liberal Arts Colleges in the United States. When I was applying for admission, I knew nothing about this highly rated college; it was not on my list. I was only interested in attending reputable, big universities in America.

As I pointed out earlier, destiny would have it that at one of the open house receptions hosted by the American Cultural Center in Lubumbashi, the American Consul could not hide his excitement and pleasure when I mentioned to him that I was admitted at Amherst, but I was still undecided and debating whether or not I should go. Enthusiastically, without a hint of reservation, he told me that it was and is one of the best schools in America and that I should go. He shared with me that he was a Williams College graduate and he had firsthand knowledge. Indeed, I would later learn about the close ties and fierce sibling rivalry that has existed between the two colleges for over 200 years, since Amherst's founding in 1821.

It was with this ringing endorsement that I rode the Greyhound bus that would take me from Washington, D.C., through Williamsport, Pennsylvania, and ultimately to the front steps of the Lord Jeff Inn in Amherst. Ready or not, I was once again facing new place and new faces. A new home.

After a few days of orientation, I was off to the races.

My class of '74 counted fewer than 300 students, all male at the time. Most classes had between twenty and thirty students, allowing for close and personal attention from professors.

I had strategically chosen my courses with a concentration in mathematics, physics, and chemistry. I had so chosen because I knew I was better prepared in these subjects and perhaps, more importantly, I would not be required to do a lot of reading.

But I also knew that I needed to continue to improve my English reading and writing skills. So, I enrolled in an introductory English course, English 11.

Top left: Waiting to catch the bus to Amherst with all my belongings in my suitcase.

Top right: Books were my first priority—freshman year, 1970.

Left: More settled and comfortable as a junior.

Kalonji, my best man, and me, 1980.

Soon after the beginning of classes, I realized that although the Language Institute at Georgetown had done a fantastic job in eight short weeks, the pace and volume of college instruction was more challenging than I had anticipated. Whereas my decision to take science classes was great, choosing a college English class almost turned into a disaster. I say "almost" because, as it is often said, "At the height of the storm there are always angels in the midst of strangers."

Professor Armour Craig, my English 11 teacher, was such an angel. Very early on he saw that I was struggling to keep up with the rest of the class and would certainly fail if left alone. I was also thinking about dropping the course to avoid such a disastrous grade on my transcript. But Professor Craig tailored the course to my ability, with fewer reading and writing assignments. I attended the classes and had many private lessons. These numerous tutoring sessions, which went beyond the call of duty for Professor Craig also became counselling sessions that tremendously alleviated my anxieties and helped me keep my eyes on the prize.

Not only did I manage through, but, with his help, I was named to the Dean's List at the end of the semester. What a big sigh of relief! I could breathe easier again, knowing then that I was going to make it. I celebrated in silence. I had thought about calling my family or at least writing them to let them know about this award, but it quickly occurred to me that they wouldn't even know what the Dean's List meant. They wouldn't appreciate the tremendous effort this endeavor required. So, as with my previous achievements in high school, I was satisfied and content to know that I was good enough to make it at one of the best schools in America.

I was back on track. And even though I was no longer first or second in all my classes, as I was accustomed to in secondary school, I remained on the honors list from that moment on.

Still putting my studies first, I found time to indulge in extracurricular activities such as soccer and mixers. I learned to drive and shortly after bought my first car. I made new friends on and off campus, including my dear friend Kalonji Kabongo, who would later become the best man at my wedding. I explored the many social and educational activities offered at the surrounding four colleges: Mount Holyoke, Smith, UMass, and Hampshire. I joined the International Student Organization and became its president in my junior year. I expanded my literary repertoire and read authors such as James Baldwin, Langston Hughes, Malcolm X, Maya Angelou, and Chinua Achebe. I reread and translated for my Black Studies Professor, Asa Davis, extracts of Frantz Fanon, Aimé Césaire, Jean-Paul Sartre, and Albert Camus. I was drawn to diverse authors but mostly to those who were exploring issues of identity, exploitation, slavery, colonization, neo-colonization, imperialism, and the like.

In the end, my liberal arts education at Amherst turned out to be truly expansive, liberating, and enlightening. With the support and encouragement of such wonderful and caring teachers such as Prof. Craig Armour (English), Prof. Ted Leadbetter (Biology), Prof. Asa Davis (Black Studies), Prof. Robert Ward (President of the College) and many others, Amherst became for me yet another home away from home. I owe to all of them a ton of gratitude.

Not only did they help me remain on the honors list, but it is with their assistance that I became a member of Phi Beta Kappa and graduated four years later with a magna cum laude in Biology.

The graduation ceremony was beautiful but emotionally anticlimactic. I was happy because I had conquered yet another challenge, but sad that none of my family nor my old friends could share in this accomplishment. I celebrated quietly as I looked forward to an upcoming vacation that four of my AAI friends and I had organized.

With a small stipend that we had received from AAI, we pulled off a most memorable summer vacation that took us from Portland, Oregon, to Tijuana, Mexico, over a six-week period. Driving packed in a rented station wagon, camping in multiple parks and alternating sleeping arrangements in cheap motels, we weaved our way down the West Coast exploring, often in amazement, many tourist sites, including Crater Lake, Napa Valley, Lake Tahoe, and Yosemite National Park. We were amazed by the majestic redwoods, rode the cable cars in San Francisco, were enthralled by the magic of Disneyland, marveled at the paradise-like setting of Monterey Bay, basked in the pleasant weather in San Diego, and had crazy fun in Tijuana with its lively bars and bustling streets.

We were unencumbered. We felt free and mostly happy to finally discover some of the beauty and diversity of the American landscape, the apparent freedoms and opportunities available in America.

Towards the end of our trip, I particularly remembered Monterey Bay, with its near-perfect climate, clean air, beautifully manicured lawns, swimming pools filled with clean blue water, and its many luxurious houses. For a brief moment, I imagined myself living there—but only briefly, because before I could settle in my dreams, a little voice quickly reminded me that I was here for a purpose and I still had miles to go before I rest.

Rochester

Just like four years earlier when destiny landed me at the doorsteps of Amherst, its hands were leading me again, but this time towards Rochester, New York. Although I longed for and would have preferred a brighter, sunnier place like Monterey—and although I had applied and was even later accepted at other medical schools, including Emory, Meharry, and Howard—the University of Rochester had offered me early admission with a full financial aid package that included scholarships and very low-interest-rate loans. The support from AAI had ended, and I had no other financial resources. So, needless to say, I followed the money.

Rochester did not have the quaintness and beauty of Amherst, especially in the fall. It did not have the vibrancy or glitz of a major city. Except for being home to such worldwide known companies like Xerox, Kodak, and Bausch & Lomb, it was rather stuck in the middle. It was quiet and often boring, bordering on dreadful at times with its cruel, gray, and cold winters. I told myself I would spend my four years, get my degree, and get out of town. And for at least the first two years, I spent most of my limited vacation time driving down I-90 back to Cambridge and Boston where I had a few friends. But for the most part, I was comforted by the knowledge that, true to my long-term goal, I came here to attend one of the most reputable medical schools in the country. And so, thankful for the opportunity, I focused on the task at hand.

By any metric or definition, medical school schedules are grueling. Ours was no exception.

It started with a shock baptism: the anatomy lab. In almost a ritual fashion, we stood next to each other in multiple rows in front of long benches holding several, cold, metal boxes that, by all appearances, looked like coffins. In unison, we were asked to open the containers and were thus briskly introduced to "our" cadaver with whom we would spend the next several weeks. The cadavers were cold and stiff, with a strong smell of formaldehyde. Yet, they were silently speaking to us about what were once warm-blooded human beings who had, generously, chosen to donate their bodies for the advancement of education and science.

I wondered later whether this ritual was designed purposely to see if we had the grit and that je ne sais quoi that is required to make it in medical school. In any case, following the initial jolt, we all gradually became not only comfortable but quite familiar with our cadavers, including their most intimate organs, muscles, nerves, blood vessels.

Other courses followed, including physiology, microbiology, and so on. We each settled in our own rigorous and demanding routines. It was a routine that required much self-discipline and left little room for misadventures or mistakes; it also left little time for extracurricular activities.

With a total of about fourteen black medical students in my four years of medical school, and only one other African student, from Liberia, we carved out small networks of support. We emotionally supported each other and encouraged each other often especially when confronting the inevitable difficult and dark days. In the prevailing climate of "affirmative action," we were all aware that we were under the microscope and had to prove ourselves at every turn.

Raphael T. Tshibangu, M.D.

We constantly fought the ever-present feeling of being impostors in the prevalent sea of white coats, students, and faculty. We knew we had to work harder, twice as hard, for the same recognition. We knew there was no excuses for any lapses since, as we also learned quite early, any error from a black student was attributed to ignorance, incompetence, or ineptitude, whereas an error from a white student was probably due to fatigue or other extrinsic factors.

With determination, we all, but one, conquered the rigors and challenges of med school and without fanfare, I graduated four years later. Regrettably, maybe because of our own individual life circumstances, but certainly not by design, my colleagues and I went our separate ways following graduation, with only the minimal of contacts over the ensuing years. To Abib Conteh, Otis Tucker, Melvin Rapalyea, Beverly Love, with fond memories, I remain grateful.

Following medical school, all of us had to choose an area of practice that was of interest, such as surgery, internal medicine, or radiology, and receive specialized training in that discipline.

It was customary for most fourth-year students to go through a matching system whereby each student ranks their choices of residency programs, which in turn ranks the students in order of preference. When the choices and preferences are matched, it is determined where the graduating medical students would train as Interns and as Residents later. This long and anxiety-provoking process is still in use today.

So it was that, as I was considering the matching process, I had already decided that a residency in obstetrics and gynecology would best serve my long-term goals. A clinical rotation in OB/GYN had crystallized this choice for me. In such a residency program I would be exposed to internal medicine and surgery, as well as multiple sub-specialties. This exposure would be necessary in the Congo, where access to many specialists is severely limited. As destiny would have it, the director of the OB/GYN residency program, Dr. Van Huysen, who had heard of my residency choices, promptly offered me a position outside of the matching system. Since I, like many other students, dreaded the agonizing wait and uncertainty of the matching system, and since by this time my feelings for Rochester had warmed up somewhat, I accepted the offer without hesitation. The reasons why Dr. Van Huysen offered me that position have remained obscure. I did not question the motives.

The Universe was unfolding.

I was relieved, in fact. I did not have to wait for the match result. I could start to internalize the idea of my residency at the University of Rochester Affiliated Hospitals, and mentally adjust to another four years in Rochester.

My residency program at the University of Rochester had its own hurdles. It involved rotations at multiple university-affiliated hospitals, which included, then, Strong Memorial, Highland, St. Mary's, and Genesee. You can imagine that being a male, black, African physician with mostly white and female patients could not have been an easy proposition. Fortunately, having the shield of a medical degree and being battled tested, I confidently embraced the challenges of my residency with only mild trepidation. As the fears and anxieties dissipated, they were replaced by more confidence and more satisfaction. I was learning more, I was becoming more knowledgeable, expanding my expertise and feeling more academically and professionally accomplished. I felt even more so in my fourth year as Chief Resident, maybe because it was becoming clear and certain that not only did I have an M.D., but I would soon become a specialist as well. I was feeling better and better prepared, more and more capable of practicing anywhere in the world. And nobody could take that away from me.

Unlike most residents, when I finished my residency, I did not look for a job in the United States. I had always planned to return home and was often offended when anybody implied otherwise. However, by 1982, twelve years after leaving, my Homeland—the Congo, then Zaire—had descended into worse chaos. A mass exodus of professionals was underway. My friends, former high school mates, and my family advised me to stay. Their own situations becoming precarious, they could not offer any kind of support, financial or otherwise, if I were to return. Companies such as Gécamines and SNCZ (formerly SNCC) were no longer able to adequately pay their employees and were no longer hiring. The hospitals had become destitute.

Given that, by this time, I had been married for two years and had a responsibility; and given that the prospects for gainful work in the Congo were less than dim, I reluctantly and with much anguish decided to follow the advice of my friends and family. I finished my residency and took a job with a reputable multispecialty medical group, Rochester Medical Group. Fortuitously, the job had been offered to me, unsolicited, a year before the end of my residency.

Never in my wildest imagination, never in the most remote recesses of my mind, could I have visualized myself living in snowbound western New York following my residency. And yet, from that moment on, Rochester, New York, would become my home.

Obviously one of the most significant moments in Rochester was our wedding, on May 10, 1980. Beautiful but simple, small, cozy. My brother Albert with Sherry and me.

With Sherry and her parents.

All work and no play? Playing guitar, dancing, water-skiing, and cross-country skiing.

Raphael T. Tshibangu, M.D.

Sherry and me, settling in Penfield, 1989.

Raphael T. Tshibangu, M.D.

On Family

Between anatomy and physiology classes, hematology and microbiology lectures, between the tedious library research projects and voluminous reading assignments, medical school and residency still afforded me a semblance of "normal" life. My normal included a quick pickup soccer game, mostly with other immigrants, a relaxing get-together with a very small group of friends, or a rare night out at a cheap restaurant, the movies, or a local nightclub.

It was on one of those occasional nights out that I first laid eyes on her. It was a summer evening. It was a calm, clear, moonlit night. My friends and I were standing outside the club about halfway between the front door and the parking lot. We were talking and people watching. There was an occasional "What's up?", "How're you doing?", "Great night!"

We were chilling, laughing, and enjoying the fresh air. We were taking a respite from the noisy, hot, and smoke-filled club ambiance. Then, exiting the club was a group of three or four young women joyfully chatting and laughing. They were clearly having fun. Among them was a noticeably beautiful gazelle: head high, chest pushed up, confident but slightly undulating gait. She was animated and clearly aware of the eyeballs glaring in her direction. She was sporting a short haircut and wearing high heels that accentuated her sculpted-brick legs that were left exposed by a semi-short, form-fitting yellow and black dress. A few "Hey, what's up?" was all we could manage to utter as they approached. They did not appear interested in us, but I gleefully noticed a furtive glance, a partially attentive look back as they went by and disappeared into the night.

Several months later, one of my friends, Jide Anjorin, invited me to dinner. He was making his famous Nigerian spicy rice with chicken, and he knew how much I longed for, and appreciated, a soulful, home-cooked African dish. Coincidentally, Jide's girlfriend had also previously invited one of her friends to the same dinner. Not planned, they told us later. It was pure coincidence.

As in previous occasions, I was only looking forward to a nice meal and quiet evening with a friend. I had no other expectation. So, you can imagine my surprise and guarded delight when I saw her again, "the beautiful gazelle," from the nightclub. A slight twinge of anxiety quickly dissipated as we were introduced and the libation started flowing.

I met Sherry that wonderful night at Mt. Hope Town House, just a few minutes away from the University campus and Graduate Living Center. We drank, ate, and laughed. There may not have been bells ringing or stars dancing that night, but, planned or not, I felt deep in my soul that she was there for me. I was comfortable and at ease. The occasion exceeded my expectations. The night ended with an affectionate touch, a warm embrace, and an exchange of telephone numbers.

Raphael T. Tshibangu, M.D.

Sherry was finishing her undergraduate studies at the university and she lived on the River Campus across the river from the Medical School, where I was also neck-deep in my own pursuits. Despite the close proximity, our contacts remained cordial but limited.

As to the details of our courtship during the subsequent years, our accounts remain somewhat blurry and sometimes discordant. Indeed, we would sometimes joke later that if we were participants in *The Newlywed Game* we would fail miserably because of our different recollections about our relationship during those subsequent years. It could have been because of her move to Atlanta to pursue an MBA, which made contact even more limited; it could have been that I was also embarking on my internship and residency, and we both needed to devote our energies towards the pursuit of our respective goals.

In any case, what I clearly remember is that during this time I began to feel and experience the cost of long-distance relationships, the cost of being away from family and close friends. It was during this time that Astrid, "Assy," my older brother Vincent's wife, died. She was my sister-in-law but also a very close friend even before her marriage to my brother. The news came as shock. It was unimaginable. She was so young and healthy, with an enviable lifestyle. The news was difficult to process because I always felt that even though I did not talk to my family regularly, I would eventually see them and talk to them face-to-face. Up until then, I had not experienced such a great and permanent loss. It was the first death in my immediate family. I did not know my grandparents, nor did I know my father's brother when they died.

Although I was able to talk and cry on the phone with my brother Vincent, for the most part I grieved alone. I thought a lot about my family then. I thought about *"La maison que J'aimais, La maison où j'ai grandi"* ("The house that I loved, the house where I grew up") by Françoise Hardy, repeated a million times: *"Je reviendrai un jour, un beau matin, parmi vos rires."* ("I will come back one day, one fine morning, among your laughter.") I thought about *Si j'avais un Marteau* (*If I Had a Hammer*) by Claude François:.

Long before I learned about the evidence-based science of music, about how music can improve respiration, lower blood pressure, increase cardiac output, relax muscle tension, and reduce stress, I enjoyed listening to different types and genres of music. Instinctively, I chose songs that helped me cope with my solitude or many other stressful, depressing, or anxiety-producing situations.

For several years, I also derived similar benefits when I dabbled in playing the guitar and the keyboard. Indeed, music was often therapeutic for me. It was sometimes soothing, sometimes inspiring and invigorating. It was, and still is, good for the soul; it is good for the mind and body.

So, it was with this cheerful and optimistic song, which I learned many years ago, in secondary school, and listened to for consolation and for validation of the hardship and isolation I was enduring. The song conveyed to me the importance and the value of hard work. As Claude Francois put it, *"Je cognerais le jour, je cognerais la nuit. J'y mettrai tout mon coeur…Oh oh, ce serait le bonheur."* ("I will hammer in the morning, I will hammer in the evening. I will put all my heart into it…Oh oh, that would be happiness.")

The song also professed his strong attachment and love for his family, declaring that "all I need is a hammer, a bell and a song, for the love of my father, my mother, my brothers and my sisters…that would be happiness."

It is not hard work for the sake of it but work to build something—work to take care of my family, my father, my mother, my brothers, and my sisters. In other words, happiness required hard work with a purpose.

This message resonated with me. It inspired me.

As I listened to those words and repeated them in my mind from time to time, I knew I was on the right path.

But for now, I told myself, I have to pay the price. I have to manage. And so, I grieved alone. For the first time since I was separated from my family many years earlier, the stress had overtaken my defenses and landed me in the hospital with a gastric ulcer.

I continued to miss my family in the Congo, but resiliently marched on. I began to have feelings about starting my own immediate family and started thinking about marriage more and more—certainly not before the end of medical school, but maybe shortly after.

I had previously discussed the topic with my brothers as well as my father. As expected, they unequivocally expressed their preference for a Congolese wife and preferably a "Muluba." Customs dictated. They made it clear on multiple occasions they were ready to start the search and vetting process. "Candidates abound," they would say. "All we need is the green light."

I, on the other hand, did not feel bound by the custom dictates and was frankly uncomfortable with the idea of an imported bride. So, when the time came, I pleaded my case convincingly and without much difficulty. Without recalling the exact words, my argument was along the line of "I already have a black—not white—American girl that I love; she is very giving, family-oriented, not brash, educated, and could even pass for Congolese." Fortunately, there was little pushback, and I can only surmise that having grown away from the village and not as strongly entrenched in the traditional wedding process, my parents and my family were understanding and deferential to my decision.

I had chosen, I had decided, I had their blessing, and Sherry accepted.

Let it be stated, however, that I appreciated the reasons why they, like many Congolese, would have preferred a non-American wife. It was often said and accepted that Americans are individualistic. Americans were known for their quest for freedom and independence, their self-reliance, and their hard work in the pursuit of personal goals. But, the widely shared impression was that they do so to the point of being selfish and egotistical, prioritizing their own self-interests as opposed to, or at the expense of, others. It was also believed and widely accepted that they preferred small families with one or two children rather than be encumbered or burdened by large, extended families.

My position, however, is that the ideas of independence and self-reliance, personal responsibility, and hard work are not antithetical to a sense of community, a feeling of unconditional belonging to a large group, and commitment to one another. Furthermore, I believe that, at its best, an extended family provides a ready-made community where culture and traditions are shared, a space where conflict resolution and shared grief or loss is carved out, and a support system that encourages and celebrates. It also provides for the load and the pain to be lightened because it is spread among many and for the joy to be enhanced as it is multiplied. There is happiness in freedom and independence, but there is also love and strength in community.

It was under that prism that I had argued that my chosen American girl was special! Not only pretty, smart, confident, and lively, she was also—most importantly—deeply grounded and rooted in her family, which included many siblings as well as aunts, uncles, and cousins. I knew this from close observation of her interactions at many different family functions I was invited to attend. I strongly believed that the profound attachment toward her extended family would also be accorded to my own family, as she effortlessly and unequivocally later demonstrated.

With no other major or insurmountable challenges, we finally made a commitment to marry on May 10, 1980.

It was a small but beautiful ceremony, held in the living room of our small house in Henrietta, New York. It was simple but cozy and warm. Except for my younger brother, Albert, who had joined me the year prior, and my best man, Kalonji Kabongo, we were surrounded mostly by Sherry's family members, including her mother, Bennie Lou; her father, Herman Haygood; her three sisters, Deretha, Madeline, and Selma; and her younger brother, Herman, as well as a couple of other relatives. On that day, her family became my family. I missed my family in the Congo, but I was happy and joyful on that special occasion.

My roots in Rochester were growing and deepening!

For many years, life events were happening for me largely in accordance with my plans and goals. But starting in August 1982, when I made the momentous and heart-wrenching decision to stay in Rochester, it became abundantly clear, as written by Robert Burns centuries ago, "The best-laid schemes of mice and men go oft awry." As we were planning our future and hoping to build our immediate family, the Universe was still unfolding in line with our intentions but not necessarily according to our plans.

A previously unsuspected medical condition would keep us from having our own biological children.

L'homme Propose, Dieu Dispose (Man Proposes, God Disposes)

In 1984, four years after marriage, I became a permanent resident and was again able to travel freely after being confined to the U.S. for lack of travel documents. Sherry was also ready to go to Zaire and finally meet and visit with my family. There was visible excitement and maybe some apprehension on her part about going to Africa, the "dark continent." The apprehension was mostly palpable in her parents, who met with us and prayed for her safe travels and return. "Come back safely," they prayed.

I had planned the itinerary to allow for a slow introduction and immersion. We stopped in Brussels and stayed with some Congolese friends for a few days. We ate Congolese food, listened to Congolese music, and spoke mostly French and Swahili. She did not mind and, in fact, appeared quite at ease. We also purchased a few Zairean outfits among which a navy blue abacost for me and a patterned yellowish wrapper and blouse with light brownish, sheer sleeves for her. She thoroughly enjoyed this short stay in Brussels and, as a result, my own anxieties about the trip were markedly alleviated.

Beautifully dressed in this Zairean outfit, Sherry left no doubt in anybody's mind that she was Zairean. From the moment we landed in Kinshasa, people would confidently address her in one of our languages before they realized by her amusingly puzzled and nonverbal reaction that she was not Zairean. As time went on, she would occasionally respond, *"Je parle français un peu,"* with a betraying American accent. Cute!

For the most part, I played the role of interpreter and, except for the frequent need for translation, we managed quite well from the start. Any anxieties we had when we started the trip quickly dissipated. It was indeed wonderful visiting with my brother Vincent and his family, my older brother Alphonse, my parents, and my extended family members as well as several old friends. It was an enjoyable and memorable trip.

Not only memorable, but unexpectedly life changing.

We were staying with my brother Vincent in Lubumbashi and were immensely enjoying our time with the kids. Unbeknownst to me, some of the kids may have expressed to Sherry their desire to live with us in America. One evening, almost on a whim, it seemed to me, Sherry suggested that we take one of my brother's little girls back with us. I thought it was a good idea and suggested that maybe we should come back at a later date, after we had made the appropriate preparations. Sherry insisted. "We have to do it now," she said. We had not previously discussed any such arrangements. We had not previously discussed adoption. We did not know how it would work. After I raised many logistical obstacles, many of which she was unaware, Sherry remained unwavering in her request. She was serious; she meant what she said and she would be happy if we could make it happen. So, without further hesitation, I agreed. A discussion with my brother and his wife, Charlotte, followed the next morning; they both agreed.

However, once the decision was made, we had to race against the clock; we did not have the luxury of time. We were already scheduled to return to the U.S. in a few days. It usually requires weeks, if not months, to obtain needed documents for travel and admission to the U.S. We had to accomplish this legally in just a matter of days. Passport, visa, vaccination card, child travel authorization, and so on. My brother and Charlotte's uncle, Dr. Ntumba, were reasonably well connected. With their assistance, we navigated our way through the migration bureau for a travel document, the clerk's office to notarize the parent's authorization letter, the travel clinic for vaccinations and a vaccination card, and the American Consulate for a visa. We accomplished all of this in record time, even though it required an occasional but customary bribe.

Against all odds, two weeks after we left the United States, we were back, accompanied by a beautiful, vivacious, slightly scared but excited young girl, Titi, legally named Kamwanya Christine Kazadi.

Our immediate family had suddenly grown by one.

We became parents overnight and had to immerse ourselves, with no warning, in parental duties and activities: finding the right school, arranging for special instructions for a non-English speaking six-year-old, arranging after-school childcare, shopping for school items, getting medical insurance. We learned relatively quickly how to provide for her basic needs, not only for her education and medical needs, her food and clothing needs, but also her emotional and psychological needs—to feel safe, for self-esteem, for family support. With the assistance of the many nephews and nieces on Sherry's side, who helped with many chores, babysitting, and mostly support and companionship for Titi, we were able to enjoy a happy family life, gladly assuming our parental responsibilities the best way we could in the face of extremely demanding jobs for both of us.

Luckily, our task was made easier by the fact that Titi did not exhibit any significant symptoms or signs of dislocation, and, on the contrary, seemed to adapt relatively fast and quite well.

Roots were getting deeper and deeper as my brother Albert also started to build his immediate family.

In 1979, Albert, who had already finished high school in Mbuji-Mayi, was vegetating at a local university. He had previously expressed his intentions to come to the U.S. to pursue his studies and obviously had the necessary academic credentials. The only challenge was getting the travel documents, which we were fortunately able to obtain once his college admission was secured. In the summer of that year, he started his own American journey.

Only a few weeks after joining us in Rochester, he began his English classes followed by his undergraduate studies at the State University of New York at Brockport. He would graduate from the same institution about four and a half years later. He then went on to get his MBA from Golden Gate University, in California.

Prior to moving to California in late 1984, which was only a few weeks after graduating from Brockport, he travelled to the Congo and met his previously vetted bride, Odette Kabongo. Following a traditional wedding, Odette, who had stayed behind due to the lack of the necessary papers, finally joined him in 1985.

After the birth of their first child, Tresor Tshimanga, nicknamed Chichi a year later, they rejoined us in Rochester where the second child, Chanelle Kamwanya (Channy), was born. It was a wonderful and joyful moment, especially since Sherry, as a supportive auntie, and I, as the uncle and delivering obstetrician, were present during her delivery.

Hence, with the arrival of their two children, Chichi and Channy, the Kalonji family nucleus was taking shape and our extended family was growing.

Our family multiplied further when our godchild, Bibish Kazadi, came to live with us in 1996, during her high school years while her parents were battling the cold in Baie-Comeau, Canada; it grew even more when my nephew Kadima Mfuamba was plucked from Mbuji-Mayi and became part of our household. Our house had indeed become a Home, noisy with the sound of laughter, warm and mostly happy.

I could rightfully call Rochester "Home."

We also shared the laughter with many friends we made and continued to make over the years. Friends with whom we enjoyed multiple social events, played games, and engaged in sporting activities such as Ping-Pong, squash, racquetball, tennis, and golf with a friendly dose of competition; friends with whom we played cards and even indulged in a little gaming for added excitement; friends with whom we have been fortunate enough to travel and vacation with around the world.

Because of their enduring permanence—a cherished gift—some of the relationships have transcended friendship and morphed into brotherhood and sisterhood. Such is the case with Swaze and Joe Kazadi, Clayton and Dorelis Osborne, Mary Anne and Herb Wolfe, David and Paulette Vickers, Winsome and Robert Carter. We have celebrated some of the most intimate and precious moments in our lives and supported each other during the inevitable painful occasions. Together, we have blissfully witnessed many births, baptisms, graduations, weddings, and now grandchildren. Together, just like an extended family.

At the same, the number of my relatives in Rochester and the U.S. at large has continued to grow. My nephew Albert Kalonji (Little Albert), was next. His wife, Michou, and children followed. More nephews, Ting Kasambayi and Douglas Kasambayi, came afterwards and they too made Rochester their home.

With the addition of their children as well as the arrival of other family members that they helped migrate from the DRC, our expanded family in the U.S. now counts more than four dozen. For the most part, this has allowed us to moderately experience and enjoy the benefit of an extended family again. Celebrations, such as Thanksgiving and Christmas, have had more meaning.

Like with most Americans, Thanksgiving became a truly family day. We would usually gather at my in-laws' house and occasionally at ours. There was the obligatory turkey, stuffing, greens, and macaroni and cheese. But there was also always the very sweet Kool-Aid punch, sweet baked beans, and my mother-in-law's sweet potato pie that we all looked forward to. There was a lot of food, a lot of noise, and a lot of laughter. After we each had a chance to update the family on major, impactful events of the year and to say what we were thankful for, we ate and ate again. We then played UNO, Trouble, Tonk, or checkers until late in the evening as people started peeling off and heading back home with their "plates to go." It was predictable but always enjoyable; predictable but good for the soul.

For Christmas, most celebrations were held at our house. They were particularly memorable in the late '90s and early 2000s, when many of the younger children in the family would stay over on

Christmas Eve and wake up the next morning with excitement and anticipation about the forthcoming gifts. The traditional gift exchange was accompanied by the usual "Aaah" and "Wooow." Sometimes semi-chaotic but always fun.

Our feast had a definite Congolese flavor. Most family members brought different dishes based on their culinary expertise. The variety of food included *foufou* (boukari), which is best eaten with one's bare hands; boiled or fried yuca (manioc), casava leaves flavored with peanuts or salted fish, seasoned fried fish, stew and spicy chicken, red beans with onions and tomatoes, and more. Needless to say, the music was mostly Congolese and often included a few Luba artists such as Tshala Muana, who magnetically pulled us to the dance floor to do the *mutuashi*, a traditional dance of the Luba people. While singing along, we would spontaneously form a circle while stepping to the rhythm of the music. Alternatively, one or two people would get in the middle of the circle to demonstrate their dancing skills, which involved a fair amount gyration around the waist. And regardless of age or skill level, it was always wonderful to watch, especially when we tied a large piece of cloth, such as a sheet or a "wrapper," around each other's waist to accentuate the hip movements.

Also wonderful—and perhaps more significant—was a Talent Show tradition we spontaneously started and would maintain for many years. During these gatherings, we encouraged everybody to participate and showcase their talent or abilities in any area of their choosing. The audience selected judges, and we provided monetary prizes. They played musical instruments, such as guitar, keyboard, saxophone; they sang contemporary music, gospel music, Congolese music; they danced; they recited poetry and told stories; they performed comedy and even magic tricks.

No doubt it was great entertainment. But soon enough Sherry and I realized that it was also a great way to awaken some of the latent gifts many of the kids had and, at the same time, instill confidence in them. In a fun and gentle way, we were encouraging them to pursue their passion. And given the importance we place on education, we took advantage of these events to also recognize and reward those students who brought in their transcripts showing a better-than-average grade.

Interestingly, at times I couldn't help but smile as I saw flashes of my father giving us an extra treat, (candy, corn, special meal), when we brought home an excellent grade.

Like most families, we had fun together; we supported each other and consoled each other whenever necessary.

Unfortunately, despite this, the plight of those who remain in the DRC has always been in our thoughts. These, often tormenting, thoughts have always been barely under the surface. We all knew that the socioeconomic conditions in the DRC were gradually and then rapidly deteriorating. With deplorable conditions spirally descending into hell, the suffering had spared no one, not even my family members. Even those who in previous years could afford many luxuries were sadly being engulfed in the nascent culture of poverty, misery, defeatism, corruption, laziness, and beggary that was drowning the entire country.

The needs were—and are—obvious, and the instinct to help is not in doubt. However, like many other immigrants, I continue to struggle with the entitlement mentality of those who were and still are in a constant state of expectancy, simply by virtue of being members of the clan. I continue to struggle, like many others, on how and what best way to help. Food and lodging, tuition and other educational needs, health care needs, funerals, weddings, and other celebrations—these were and still are some of the reasons for hundreds or thousands of trips to Western Union and MoneyGram agencies. I continue to struggle, with many attempts at creating employment: leveraging old friends' connections and creating small businesses, from real estate to transportation, small retail shops, and even a try at diamond trading.

I am still struggling and will probably continue to do so until I figure out the best way to help. It has not been easy so far, since, at times, it feels like throwing money in a bottomless pit while wondering with anguish if I am truly helping or simply enabling victimization and perpetuating the entitlement mentality.

Several times, in my dark moments, I felt like given up on my DRC family.

One such time was shortly after the death of my father, in 1995. It was sudden and unexpected, passing away peacefully in his sleep. I felt like I had lost my anchor. I felt like I had not done enough for him or my family. I remembered Claude François's "If I had a hammer" and I wondered where I had fallen short. I remembered Françoise Hardy and her "the house I loved" and wondered how the landscape would be with him not around. At the same time, I was inexplicably disheartened by the fate of my family, as they seemed to be totally incapable of fending for themselves. I wanted to continue to help, but I did not want to continue to enable bad and destructive behaviors.

I am thankful for my family. "In times of test, family is best." In back (left to right): Sherry's siblings Deretha, Herman, Madeline, Napoleon, Sherry; In front (left to right): Nephews and nieces: Nate, Joseph, Mona, Fiona; Mother-in-law holding Sharee, and Father-in-law.

Sherry and me, around 1999.

Sherry and me with my mother (left) and my mother-in-law, 1996.

With nephews Cocco, Alain, Papy, Raphael, and Joe; Capetown, South Africa, 2006.

My niece Noella's kids, Jay and Barbara, with me; Kinshasa, about 1998.

Good times are better when shared with family. In back: Chichi, Sherry, Gode, Jean-Luc, Odette, Jerry, me; In front: Raphael, Rody, Deborah; Christmas event, 2002.

Sharing a sunny afternoon in Hamilton, Canada, before a nephew's wedding, 2019.

A joyous occasion (below), 2009.

They are grown now and still growing, but in our hearts they will always be our precious babies. Above: Bibish (left) and Titi; Right: Titi (left) Bibish with Sherry and me, 1999.

Left: Douglas and family; Rochester, 2013.

Right: Nephews Albert, Ting, Douglas, and their kids, 2009.

Below: Ting and kids at Titi and Thomas's wedding, 2009.

Sherry and me with newlyweds Titi and Thomas, 2009.

A proud father with the new bride.

Odette and Albert with newlyweds Reana and Chichi (a.k.a. Trey), 2018.

With Jerry Kasambayi (grand), Jerry Ntumba (grand), and Chanelle (niece), 2009.

Travelling and creating memories. Granny with Danny and Elena; Ibiza, Spain, 2019.

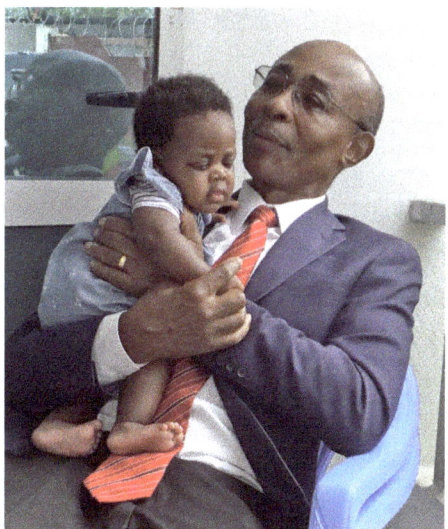

Clockwise from top left: Sherry and me with Bibish's son Luke, 2019; with Mailikiya in Kinshasa, 2019; Elena and me, 2019; Aimee Kazadi and me in Portland, Maine, 2018.

Diane Biata Kalonji, Sherry, and Rebecca with the great-grands; Pittsford, 2018.

Sherry, Titi, Elena, Danny; Slovenia, 2017.

We also try to maintain a modicum of tradition whenever possible. Rochester family at Diane's traditional wedding; Greece, New York, about 2011.

Another such dark moment was in 2000, following the death of my dear friend and soul brother, Celestin. His death affected me profoundly and for a long time.

I still remember that nice, summer day. I was dressed in a fine tailored grey suit, a white shirt, and a red tie with silver undertones. Black shoes were shining on my feet. I had just finished my office consultations and was coming home. My wife was in France, where she planned to spend several weeks studying French. My daughter was home on summer vacation. She greeted me at the door with a somber face. "Did you hear?" she said.

Worried by the soft, somber tone in her voice and her consoling face, I said, "Hear what?"

"Tonton Celestin died," she muttered. "Pamela"—his daughter—"called and she also left a message on the answering machine."

I do not remember what else she may have said, but I do remember walking away from the kitchen area where we had been standing. I headed to the bedroom down the hall and back through the kitchen to my study and back again. I did not know what to do then. I could not believe it and did not fully accept his death for many years. Long after my trip to South Africa, where he was then residing, I could not believe that he was taken away so prematurely. A General in the Congolese Armed Forces and a Minister in the government for a brief time, he was always fighting to improve the lot of his fellow Congolese. He had tried to do his best in the most turbulent times. Inexplicably, he represented my dreams and hopes for the country. And I could not believe those dreams and hopes had been so suddenly dashed. As a matter of fact, on several occasions, I would find myself in a secret location talking to my sister-in-law (his wife, Bernadette), and he would show up in different disguises and reassure us that he was still alive. He was in hiding, waiting for the appropriate time to come back and steady the ship. Of course, these were only recurrent dreams.

Those days I also felt like giving up on the country that showed no signs of redemption and seemed bent on remaining incorrigibly corrupt, chaotic, and condemned to its downward spiral.

Indeed, many of my visits to the DRC were followed by overwhelming ambivalence and mixed feelings. The visits gave me solace and joy, reconnecting with my family and my old friends. They also soothed any nostalgia I still carried about what was good in, and about, the country. They were good for the soul. At the same time, I was often sad and disappointed, disheartened about how low my family's lot had fallen and let down by the country that held so much promise. I was so sad to leave, but sometimes almost selfishly relieved that I did not have to endure that mess and the hardship.

After one such visit, I even questioned if it was worth visiting again. It was in August 2006. The main impetus for our visit was to pay respects to my brother Vincent, who had passed away the previous year in July. He had always been full of energy, determination, and hope. He was one of the first engineers in the Congo. He was one of the first Congolese executives at Gécamines. He was the pride of our family, a pillar of the clan. Unfortunately, after putting up a good fight and reaching the highest heights in his brilliant career, he prematurely succumbed to complications of adult-onset diabetes at the age of fifty-eight. He was mainly a victim of poor or nonexistent medical care.

Because of political unrest, I could not safely travel to the Congo for my brother's funeral. The presidential campaigns and elections often froth with violence and unanticipated troubles. Therefore,

Sherry and I felt it would be prudent to schedule our trip after the elections when the air would hopefully be clear. We planned to travel sometime after the July 30 elections. This would actually turn out well, because we could then participate in the customary one-year Going Home celebration as well as the installation of the tombstone. The elections took place as scheduled, but unpredictably, the final results were not to be announced until Sherry and I had arrived, about three weeks later. There was widespread belief in the country that the election was rigged, as rampant evidence of fraud and irregularities were uncovered. Jean-Pierre Bemba, the main opposition leader, vowed to challenge the results, which gave victory to Joseph Kabila, the incumbent. So, as we landed in Kinshasa on August 14, the Independent Electoral Commission (CEI) was reporting only partial results. It would announce the final results in a matter of days.

Our family and friends, including Jean Claude and Bernadette, felt that if there were to be any violence, clashes would occur mostly between the civilian supporters of the two rivals. The "skirmishes" would probably occur outside of Kinshasa or maybe in the outskirts of town, since the center of the city was fortified by a heavy United Nations Mission in the Democratic Republic of Congo (MONUC) presence. Friends and family therefore advised that it would be prudent to be back in Kinshasa at the time of the final announcement. It would be safer, especially since we were going to stay in a secure downtown neighborhood where most diplomats and ambassadors reside.

With that advice in mind, we traveled to Lubumbashi, where we had a dignified and soul-healing Home Going celebration for my brother. We were relieved and satisfied. Our mission was accomplished, uneventfully.

Two days later we were back in Kinshasa, hoping to spend a few quiet days before heading back. The next day, we noticed that the usually crowded streets and bustling markets were largely deserted as shops closed early and people rushed home in anticipation of the CEI's proclamation. The announcement came that evening, August 20, as we were finishing our dinner at Bernadette's apartment. Kabila was the victor, according to the CEI. Bemba and his supporters were predictably furious.

As we started to clear the table, we looked at each other as we heard shots in the distance. My nephew Yves, Bernadette's son, tried to be reassuring and nonchalantly explained, "Firecrackers! I am sure Kabila's supporters are celebrating." We heard a more distant "tat, tat, tat." "Relax," said Yves again, "those are just firecrackers." A few minutes later, a loud "Boom!" was followed by the unmistakable sound of machine gun. "Get down!" Yves shouted, as we all suddenly realized that far from being firecrackers, these were obvious sounds of heavy artillery and machine-gun fire. A battle had broken out and it was right in our neighborhood and near our apartment building. We pulled the ever-inquisitive Sherry from the window where she was trying to peak outside and retreated to a small room in the middle of the apartment.

From that moment on, our quiet, anxious, and somber conversations were frequently interrupted by recurrent machine-gun fire. We would later learn that forces loyal to Kabila were trying to neutralize Bemba's forces. So, contrary to what most people expected, the fighting was fiercest around Bemba's residence, which was close to where we decided to stay under the false belief that it would be safer.

We spent the night mostly awake, fully dressed, in a single room away from the windows and hallways. The next morning, we called the American Embassy where we had previously registered, hoping for a quick evacuation. We were curtly told, "We are not evacuating yet. We know where you are. Stay put. We will come for you if necessary." Not exactly the message that Sherry or I wanted to hear. Repeated calls throughout the day and the next yielded the same answer. We were getting more anxious and feeling out of control. The following day, a dozen diplomats and ambassadors—including William Swing, the chief of MONUC, trapped in Bemba's residence when the fighting broke out—were safely rescued and evacuated by UN forces. We saw a glimmer of hope as we witnessed the convoy whisk by our building. Alas, hope quickly faded and turned into disappointment and even slight anger when it was clear that the cavalry did not come for us. We remained pinned down, trapped in our little shelter. At least we had enough food, which we ate mostly in the stairwell. We had water; we were in communication with our friends and family; we were relatively safe.

We heard of a cease-fire on the third day. We heard that the airport, which was closed to all flights, would reopen for a short time to allow people, mostly expatriates, to get out of Dodge. I quickly engaged the services of Paul Sutcha, my niece Noella's husband, who was a relatively well-connected attorney in Kinshasa. Early morning on August 23, he called with very good news. "We have two seats available tomorrow on a flight to Johannesburg. It is costly," he added.

"Friends are Angels who lift us to our feet when our wings have trouble remembering how to fly." "Good friends are like stars, you don't always see them, but you know they're always there." Left to right: Cele, Sherry, Bernadette; Pittsford, 1997.

Sherry and me with Paulette and David Vickers, 2005.

Sherry and me with Dorelis and Clay Osborne; year-end reception, about 2000.

Left to right: Sherry, me, Annina, Renée; Pittsford, about 2002.

Left to right: me, Clay Osborne, Sherry, Herb and Mary Anne Wolfe, Dorelis Osborn, Julie Lane-Hailey and Craig Boatman; New Year's Eve 2014.

Winsome and Robert Carter, 2010.

Joe Kazadi and me.

Swaze Kazadi and me.

Jean Claude and Dorcas; Hotel du Fleuve, Kinshasa, 2019.

"We will take them," I said without hesitation. The price was $1,000 per ticket, and $2,000 to bump two passengers off the plane. Luckily, I had enough cash on hand, which was necessary for such an off-the-books transaction. After an interminable wait, we took the first flight the next day and, two and a half hours later, landed safely in Johannesburg, South Africa. While there, we learned that thirty to forty people had died during the fighting. What a tragedy! What a mess!

Thankfully, we escaped relatively easily and without any physical harm. We were finally able to exhale. We were even able to laugh, especially when I remarked to Sherry, "Thank God for corruption, eh?"

With a quirk in her smile, she replied, "Not funny. Not yet."

The international airport remained closed for another week after our extrication.

Back in Rochester on August 26, safe and sound, I somberly, silently asked myself if I would ever go back. Is it time to throw in the towel?

Yet, each time I felt like giving up, Sherry would nudge me to remain true to my values, to be thankful for what we have, and to continue to help whenever possible, despite some unintended results. She would help me recalibrate my expectations. She would often remind me that I have opportunities that others did not; that we should be glad and thankful that we are in a position to help. She would also say that when you help someone, you may never know how impactful your assistance may be; some of the help may be squandered and some may be life changing. She would often quote or give me a version of Luke 12:48: "To whom much is given, much is required."

The words and sentiments she expresses resonate with me spiritually and emotionally. Deep down, I know we are really on the same wavelength. And I am thankful that when I have experienced the troughs from time to time, she has been there to pull me back to the crest of the wave.

As a matter of fact, I have been back to the Congo several times since that event. So far, Sherry has not gone back with me. I have traveled by myself, with less and less trepidation.

For now, I am sure I will not forget my extended family in the DRC. I will not give up on the Congo. I will continue to assist financially, with occasional grumbling, while I continue to search for the best way to help.

On Guilt

I was in Parkland, Florida, on this particular day in mid-January 2020. It was a pleasantly warm and sunny weekday afternoon. I was lazily fidgeting with my phone when it rang. I recognized my brother Albert's phone number and quickly touched the green answer icon.

"Hey, what's up?"

"Nothing… Not much."

I knew there was something, since, because of his work schedule, we usually talked on weekends or late evenings. After exchanging greetings and a few pleasantries, he said, "I wanted to let you know that Aimee, one of our sisters, is trying to reach you."

"I know," I said.

"She said she called over a dozen times and you are not picking up."

"I know," I repeated.

He continued. "She is wondering why; she can tell that you're online and looking at WhatsApp."

"What?" I exclaimed, surprised and then quickly amused. I had not realized until then that she, like many others, could indeed tell when I was available online. I was caught in the web of technological advances.

In the past, I could deliberately ignore such phone calls. They were made through landlines and I could always tell my callers that I was not home and did not listen to my answering machine. With the advent of cellular phones, even those in the villages can easily find us.

I told my brother that I did not pick up because I knew why she was calling. It's always the same stories, always ending with a request for one thing or another. I was not ready to address whatever the needs were and did not feel like saying "no" again. He understood, as we had discussed the issues of guilt and how we have each tried to manage them. So we laughed instead.

We laughed even more when I reminded him of an extreme example of guilt avoidance.

KT, a good friend of mine, is a successful businessman with activities in the major cities of Mbuji-Mayi, Lubumbashi, and Kinshasa. He had lived in Mbuji-Mayi most of his life. That is where he started, had his headquarters, and where most of his large extended family lives.

Shortly after his relocation to Lubumbashi in early the 2000s, I asked him why he made such a move, considering the recurrent tensions between the Baluba and the natives of Katanga known as Katangase, which led to the ethnic cleansing of the Baluba in 1991–1993. With a slight grin he shared his story. He told it in minute details and for a long time; he gave a clear impression that he was finally ready to confess and in need of absolution:

> I was overwhelmed and overstressed. I have a huge family. Beside my own nine children, I have at least 100 relatives and their kids who call on me. Whenever there is a celebration or crisis—for weddings, births, tuitions, hospitalizations, funerals—I am expected to contribute in a significant way. Over time, calls for help went far beyond these occasional circumstances, and I became responsible for providing food and shelter, not just to family members, but to some friends and their relatives. It became too much. So I started screening calls. I severely limited access to the house, thanks to the ubiquitous metal gates. I instructed the house sentinels to tell anybody who shows up at the gate uninvited that I was not home.
>
> This did not help much. The calls were unrelenting. And the more they called, the guiltier I felt. I started to experience insomnia, headaches, and gastrointestinal problems, which got even more exacerbated when some family members accused my wife of keeping me from helping them the way they expected to be helped.
>
> When medical interventions proved to be insufficient, I became more spiritual. My wife and I started to pray every day, and I could tell that my symptoms began to improve but did not dissipate until later.

> During one of my business trips to Lubumbashi, I saw this five-bedroom house that was for sale. Without any previous planning, I bought the house on the spot; paid cash, including the furniture.
>
> When I returned to Mbuji-Mayi, I informed my wife that we had to move for our sanity and we are going to move immediately. We did not tell anybody.
>
> So, literally overnight, we packed several suitcases and the entire family boarded the next early morning flight from Mbuji-Mayi to Lubumbashi.

Now, he usually laughs as well when he recounts this story about skipping town in the dark of the night to run away from and avoid the constant feelings of guilt and resentment.

He still gets calls and requests, but not as many. The headaches, insomnia, and GI distress have subsided. And when I ask how he is now managing his guilt about not helping enough or resenting the demands that are placed on him, he simply says, "I do the best I can; that is all I can do. The rest, I leave up to God to deal with."

This is the same response I have heard when I have discussed this topic with many friends who are relatively well-to-do and inevitably face similar challenges. "We do the best we can, with and by the grace of God."

Dealing with guilt, living a guilt-free life is a challenge that many immigrants face, regardless of their accomplishments or their station in life.

Those who have come as refugees, running away from wars to seek a better place, often ask themselves why they were lucky to survive and make it, while others did not. They sometimes ask if and why they were deserving and they wonder if they could have anything to help those who stayed behind. These questions and feelings often lead to different manifestations and degrees of survival guilt.

Others, like me, who left under less dire circumstances and came here voluntarily looking for educational and/or economic opportunities to improve our lot may not have "survival guilt" but are not spared this internal turmoil. Even when the intentions are to assist those left behind, the questions of guilt still linger. Many of us wonder, from time to time, why, out of so many others in our family, our school, our community, we happen to be the chosen ones. We sometimes even blame ourselves for others' misfortunes and irrationally take responsibility for their misery because we somehow believe there must have been something we could have done differently and that we did not do enough.

We also often feel guilty and, if not ashamed, at least disturbed when it may appear like we are overindulging and are then reminded of those close to us who are still lacking. Such is the case with me sometimes when faced with spending a few hundred dollars for a round of golf when just a few moments earlier I had denied a request for the same amount of money from one of my relatives or a friend in need.

I am reminded of another striking, conscious—or maybe subconscious—expression of guilt that occurred several years ago. This incident helped me reexamine my own feelings and develop and adopt coping strategies.

My friend SI had hastily travelled from the Congo to the U.S. It was an extremely difficult time to travel because of civil unrest and because his leadership at work was imperative. But one of his daughters was getting married in Chicago. He had to be there.

It was a beautiful traditional ceremony where the dowry from the groom's family is presented and accepted by the bride's family, thereby joining together the two families. As is customary, this important ritual is followed by food, music, and dancing of course. Everybody seemed to be enjoying the festivities and loudly having fun. As most of us were crowding the dance floor, SI remained seated most of the evening. When Sherry asked him to dance, he reluctantly accepted. "How can I have fun when my people are suffering and dying?" he said.

He repeated the same words to me later when the music and the noise had quieted down and we were having a tête-à-tête. He felt guilty, not sure if he made the right decision, if he should have left his team in a precarious situation, even though he was going to rejoin them in just a few days. He did not feel like he deserved to dance and have fun while the others could not.

All I could offer then was, "I understand, but this is your daughter's wedding!" I could not come up with any words of wisdom or any more comforting or helpful advice.

Now, more than twenty years later, I know I can say more than restate the obvious, I can be more helpful, I can do better, thanks to the lessons I have learned over time.

I have indeed experienced many faces of guilt, from minor, passing twinges to gut-wrenching, stress-inducing, and depression-causing punches. I still remember when one of my family members died many years ago. I was talking to one of my brothers who was incoherently telling me what had transpired. At one point, in his grief, he said, "Why didn't you call to check on her? What kind of doctor are you?" I don't know what prompted such hurtful statement, but I am sure he did not realize what devastating impact it would have on my psyche.

Nonetheless, all of sudden, my grief was compounded by shame and guilt because I felt for at least a while that I could have called more often, I could have done something, I could have prevented it.

Although not as emotionally hurt as I was that first time I unexpectedly heard those words, I have had intermittent flashes of "What good are you for? If you are that good, how come you are not doing enough?" particularly when both of my parents died and when my two brothers died of what I knew to be treatable conditions.

Another unrelated but impactful experience was in January 2010 when Haiti suffered a devastating magnitude 7.0 earthquake that affected three million people, with 250 dead and over a million and a half displaced. This natural disaster resulted in the greatest humanitarian crisis in the country's history. For a long time, many Haitians could not even refer to it as an earthquake and found it acceptable in their shocked mind to simply call it "The Incident." While the earthquake struck, we happened to be right next door, in the Dominican Republic, on a much-needed and deserved winter vacation. We stayed at one of the Lifestyle Holidays Vacation Club (LHVC) properties, which offered opulence, beautiful unspoiled beaches, and an assortment of gourmet restaurants. Throughout the time we were availing ourselves of all conceivable amenities at LHVC, I could not help but think from time to time about what was going on next door in Haiti and wonder about the fairness of it all. I had twinges of guilt.

Still another experience, perhaps more interesting than meaningful, was on the occasion of a charity fundraising event where raffle tickets were sold and prizes awarded during the dinner reception. Luck would have it that I won three of the five major prizes. While I was getting up to walk to the floor to collect my third prize, I heard some gasps of disbelief and heard somebody say, "You! Again?" I could not believe it either and for a fraction of a second I thought, "Why me?" It was a slight feeling of guilt. Slight and passing, but not too dissimilar from the feeling I occasionally get when I think I may be a recipient of undeserved abundance. So, I may have been undeserving this particular time, but I grinned and collected the prize anyway.

There have been many more experiences, many manifestations and many shades of guilt from "Why me? Am I deserving? Is it fair?" to "Should I be indulging? Am I doing enough?"

Throughout and through these experiences, I have evolved emotionally. I have learned that, on one hand, a measured amount of guilt, just like a small dose of anxiety, is not only acceptable but can also be leveraged as a motivator to do something important, necessary, or worthwhile; on the other hand, too much of it will rob me of chances to have joy and happiness. It can be paralyzing; it can lead to depression, more anxiety, or worse.

Therefore, I have made a deliberate effort to minimize the level and frequency of guilt I have to manage, fully cognizant that waves will occur as I respond to the different events. To that effect, while acknowledging my self-determined obligations, I try not to take responsibility or blame for *all* the evil and bad things in the world. I try not to deal with the fairness or unfairness of life, but deal with things as they really are and try to change them for the better wherever and whenever I can. This means that I will not dwell on things I cannot control, but focus on what I can influence, change, and improve.

I have also learned that there are literally a million things that are worthwhile doing, that time and resources are limited commodities. It has become clearer and clearer that because of these limitations, it is imperative for me to prioritize my involvement in competing yet worthy causes or activities. And, in this endeavor, I have determined to let my values, my strengths, and my skills be my guide.

It is with this gradually gained awareness that, in 2010, while in the Dominican Republic, I made a deliberate decision that rather than lament or feel guilty about the "Incident," I would enjoy my vacation and at a later date go assist the people of Haiti as a healthcare provider. Once my decision was crystallized, I was able to enjoy the rest of my trip relatively guilt free. Three weeks later, I was in Léogâne, a brutally devastated port town located about twenty miles from the capital, Port-au-Prince. I spent two extremely rewarding weeks pitching in wherever I was needed at a local clinic. I even delivered a few "earthquake" babies!

This Dominican Republic–Haiti experience showed me that there should be no shame in having fun and having joy. What is required is balance. A healthy balance that allows me to stay true and loyal to my values but not martyr myself in the process.

Other experiences have also taught me that self-care is an essential element in the quest for balance. I must admit that for many years I did not entirely practice what I preached. When some patients told me that they did not have enough time to have their check-up exams, screening tests, exercises, or general healthcare because they had to take care of their husband, their parents, or their kids, I would usually reply that they would take better care of others if they were healthier and able to perform at their best. Recently, I have decided to follow my own advice. I have prioritized activities that contribute to better mental and physical health, such as meditation, yoga, and regular stretching exercises. I have also improved my nutrition, in addition to these activities that de-stress me and/or give me pleasure.

In other words, since that utterance of "What kind of doctor are you?", since my conversation with SI who chose to deny himself joy because others were suffering, and since my exchange with KT who initially chose avoidance and physical distance from his family to deal with his emotional turmoil and finally found some respite in spirituality, I have recalibrated my "guilt meter." It has not been a momentary, once-and-done decision, but rather more of a journey. Although I may not have achieved everything I set out to do, to live regret free and guilt free, I am doing the best that I can. Rather than guilt or regret, I try to live the life given to me here and now, with gratitude.

I presume that this is what my friend KT meant when he succinctly confessed to me that day a long time ago, "We do the best we can, with and by the grace of God."

I thought a lot about establishing a clinic in the DRC. I settled for lending a hand here and there. With Dr. Ntumba, in front of his clinic, 2008.

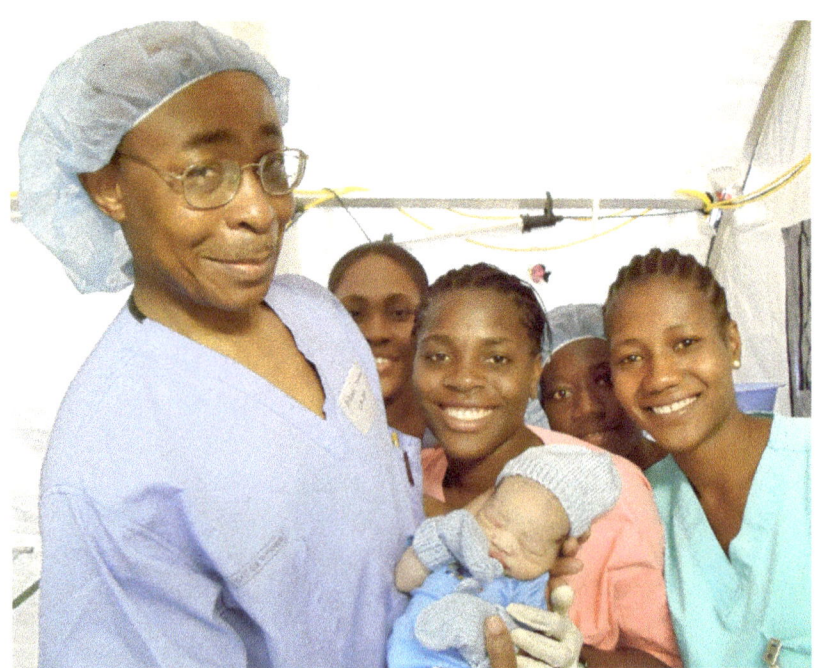

There is a lot of truth to the saying, "To be happy is to do good." With "an earthquake baby" and Haitian nurses; Léogâne, Haiti, 2010.

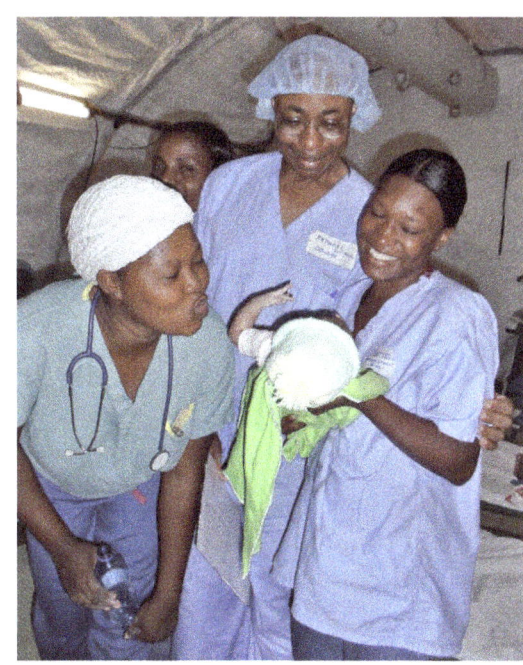

Welcoming another baby into the world (right), consulting with an expecting mother and a Haitian nurse in a makeshift clinic; Haiti 2010.

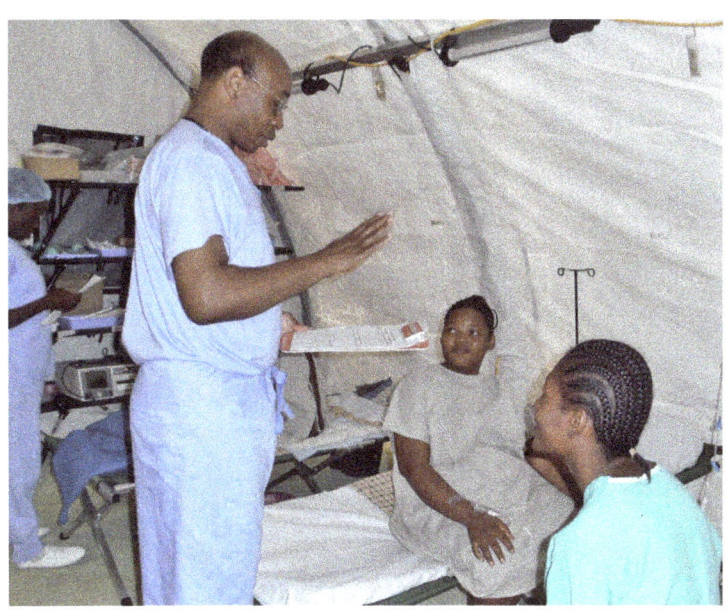

ENLIGHTENED LOYALTY

I AM A MULUBA, A CONGOLESE, AN AMERICAN, A GLOBAL CITIZEN. I do not need to deny one to belong to another. Loyalty to one of my many parts does not imply disloyalty or denial of the others. Loyalty does not mean blind allegiance or love, and criticism or disagreement does not imply disloyalty.

Walter A. Ewing, in *Immigrant Experiences,* writes about why immigrants come to America and what they find when they get here. Many are tired of living in fear and are running away from wars or government persecution and oppression; many are tired of living from hand to mouth and are running away from drought and famines; many still are just tired of being poor and want to climb the ladder of success. These statements are true, in general. They all certainly apply to many Congolese immigrants.

A recent review of Congolese migration flows by Marie-Laurence Flahaux, from the International Migration Institute, and Bruno Schoumaker, professor of demography at the University of Louvain in Belgium, demonstrate that the presence of Congolese migrants in Western countries has significantly increased over the recent decades. Starting in the 1960s, following independence, overseas migrants were going mostly to Belgium, the *metropole*. They were mostly members of the country's elite who traveled there to study or for professional training. They then returned to the Congo after completing their education or at the end of their missions. Since the mid-nineties, however, with the advent of the Rwandan Civil War in 1994 and its genocidal misadventures in the eastern Congo, thousands of Congolese migrants have arrived in Western countries, including Belgium, France, the UK, Italy, Germany, Canada, and the United States.

We have seen—and continue to see—how the northeastern part of the DRC has been devastated over the past twenty years. A bunch of murderous thugs, recruited and armed by multinationals such as Glencore, Rio Tinto, and Freeport McMoRan, with the complicity of Rwanda, Uganda, and Western allies, continue to terrorize the Great Lakes Region and to cause mayhem, chaos, death, and displacement. They have continued to operate in broad daylight, with the tacit knowledge and encouragement of these greedy multinationals. These conglomerate multinationals find it more expedient and cheaper to maintain chaos so that they can continue to exploit, plunder, pillage, steal with impunity. They were and are doing so under the watchful eye, more like "protection," of the UN's MONUSCO, which has been in the Congo with its largest contingency of over 22,000 soldiers/personnel, supposedly to maintain peace and protect the population. These heart-wrenching accounts and documentary evidence are painfully detailed by Jason Stearns in *Dancing in the Glory of Monsters,* Charles Onana in *Ces Tueurs Tutsi: Au coeur de la tragédie congolaise,* Africa Watch publications, U.N. Mapping Report 2002–2020, and many others.

At the same time, so-called Congolese leaders were also looking out mostly for their own personal interests. Some of my friends were referring to them as "looters-elite," "impostors," and "opportunists." They were constantly jockeying for power and thus enabling the thieves by contributing to the mayhem. In their cowardly, pathetic, and shallow attempts to pacify the region, we incredulously witnessed some of the gang leaders being appeased by integrating them in the Congolese Army with lofty ranks of Colonel or General.

With such a dire situation—and given the toothless, useless, and corrupt government—it is no wonder that refugees and asylum seekers represent now the majority of the Congolese obtaining permanent visas for the U.S. It is estimated that only thirty percent of migrants to the U.S. have come in via the Diversity Immigrant Visa Program or other means. Those numbers were even smaller under the Trump Administration policies.

Unlike many of the early Congolese migrants, I did not come from a privileged background of a few elites who could afford to pay for their kids' travels, tuition, and other education expenses. Unlike many of the more recent migrants, I was not running from famine due to drought; I was not running away from war, oppression, or persecution; I was not running away in search of Paradise. No, the Congo was Home for me. It was with certainty of purpose and a single-minded focus and determination that I embarked on my journey to the USA. America, the land of opportunity, was not a destination for me, it was not a heavenly resting place; rather, it was a pit stop, a way station on my life journey.

Even though, to my sixteen-year-old mind, life in the Congo was at times like Albert Camus's mythical Oran, the Congo was still Home.

Raphael T. Tshibangu, M.D.

In Oran, it seemed like the plague was always present—often dark, bleak, gloomy, and ravaging. At times dormant, to reluctantly allow for a few rays of sunshine to pierce through its always lurking and menacing clouds, it remained always threatening. Similarly, the plagues in the Congo (malaria, typhoid fever, tuberculosis, cholera, hunger, famine, wars, and more recently HIV/AIDS and Ebola) are always present, mercilessly striking, maiming, and killing many indiscriminately—and sometimes, incomprehensibly, miraculously sparing others.

Despite this scourge, the Congo was unquestionably home, and because of it, I was determined to become Dr. Rieux. His role in Oran was in line with whatever values I had espoused then, and it suited me just fine. Next to my father, Dr. Rieux was my idol. He had many of the attributes I wanted to emulate, under similar circumstances. He was neither a hero nor a saint; he was just a man with some gained knowledge, a loving heart, and compassion for his fellow men. Agnostic as he was, he did not dwell on the whys of things. He did not waste precious time wondering why things are the way they are: Why this? Why us? Why them? Why here? He was simply willing to do his best to alleviate the rampant and never-ending suffering of his fellow man. And even though he could have left Oran, despite the quarantine, he had chosen to stay and do what he could.

So, mine was not an escape from fictional Oran. I saw my journey as a temporary leave of absence in search of knowledge that would allow me, like Rieux, to combat diseases and reduce premature and preventable deaths. I was in search of knowledge that would allow me to help stamp out poverty, hunger, untold suffering, and miseries that have plagued and continue to afflict many Congolese.

As I saw it at age sixteen, my path was clear and the outcome a certainty. It would take time for sure, but I had no doubt I could and would do the work. I would pursue my education overseas; I would become a qualified and competent doctor; I would return home; I would help alleviate the suffering. Like Claude Francois, with my hammer, I would build a compound for my family—*that* would be happiness!

It was not naivete, blind optimism, or arrogance. Somehow, I just knew deep down that I wanted to become doctor and I knew deep down that I would return back home to the Congo.

It was the late '60s. Our impressions of America, based on limited knowledge gained from news magazines, the BBC, and Voice of America, were universally positive. Many of us in my small circle were dazzled and touched by the unselfish, altruistic, and generous, humanitarian work of the Peace Corps volunteers. We were inspired by Dr. Martin Luther King and the Kennedys. We swayed to the music of Otis Redding and danced to the beat of James Brown.

For most us at the time, America was portrayed as the land of milk and honey, where everything glittered. Streets were paved with gold and skyscrapers were so tall they almost peaked into heaven. It was the "land of opportunity," the land of plenty where there was no longer any poverty. We saw—more like imagined—everybody with a full belly, a big house, and one or more cars in the garage.

Who would not want to live in such a place?

Needless to say, when I announced that I was on my way to America in early 1970, many of my friends and family were happy for me. Unfortunately, some were clearly and openly envious if not ill-wishing.

Raphael T. Tshibangu, M.D.

It was also understandable that once I arrived in America, many unquestionably assumed that I would want to stay. They, too, could not imagine anybody doing otherwise, let alone going back—to where, the Congo? This often-expressed assumption, even though understandable at some level, was at times deeply offensive to me because it was so contrary to my deepest, profound, and heartfelt intentions. I would sometimes silently and sometimes openly say, politely but occasionally with exasperation and annoyance, "No, not everybody wants to stay in America. Of course I am going back." It was inconceivable for me in those early days to even imagine staying in America after my studies. How could they think, even suggest, that I should stay? Frankly, those utterances were baffling to me, as they were totally against the path I had laid out for myself. I remained undeterred as I began to attribute some of these statements to ignorance or arrogance on the part of my interlocuters who seemed to be saying to me, "This is Paradise. Why do you want to go back to Hell?"

As a matter of fact, at every reception, party, mixer, or small gathering, when faced with questions such as "What is your major? What do you want to do after college? Are you going back to Africa?" I was often amazed but also amused that a lot of my classmates had no idea about what they wanted to do after college. They were having a tough time deciding which major to choose, not to mention what they were going to do upon graduation. They were in school because that was what everybody else did. They were going through the motions. They would figure it out later. How immature, I often thought.

Can't Let Go

I was also amazed, and sometimes slightly offended, at how clueless some of them were about the world outside of the United States and how ignorant many were about the Congo in particular. "Where is the Congo?" I often heard. "It's a small town in Louisiana," I sometimes joked waiting in vain for a corrective response.

How could they be so America-centric and so ignorant? They don't even know where Africa is on the map, let alone the Congo, which is at the heart of Africa and is the size of New England. And so, rather than being embarrassed that so many people had no knowledge about Africa and had no idea where the Congo was, I gradually became comforted by the thought and realization that I knew more than they did. I could name all of the states in the United States, all the capitals, and most of the major cities. Obviously, I knew where the Congo who was on the map!

I only wished then that the questions would stop; but alas, I would continue to hear many references to Tarzan and the *Adventures of Tin-Tin*. I continued to endure many questions about lions, elephants, and gorillas. Some, even wondered out loud, how it is to live in a tree house, if one is not lucky enough to afford a mud hut.

Prior to my arrival at Amherst, I had been running full throttle, straightforward, without hesitation. I was full of confidence. I started running when I was separated from my family and chose to stay in school rather than return to Mbuji-Mayi with my parents; I was running when I went to boarding school at Karavia; I was running when I rushed to Kinshasa to work on my travel documents, not even waiting for my high school graduation ceremony; I was running when I took my first overseas flight by myself and took the dreaded transatlantic flight to New York City; I was running when

I found myself a few days later at Georgetown University for my intensive English course; I was running when ten weeks later I officially became a freshman at one of the best small Ivy League schools in America. I was running, not from the Plague, but in search of an antidote. It may have appeared to some that I was running away from a house on fire, but I knew, without a shadow of a doubt, that I was running to fetch some water to help put out the fire.

Even in my dreams, I would often run. At times I would even fly—wingless, but I would fly nonetheless—fly for fun, but mostly fly towards my goal. I was on automatic.

So, when the questions started coming incessantly—sometimes innocently and sometimes maliciously—there was no wavering in my decision. Instead, interestingly enough, during those early years, my determination to go back home only grew exponentially. I was even more resolute, especially with the advent of civil rights grievances, marches, and demonstrations, which caused America's luster to fade somewhat in my eyes.

Gradually, America's past as well as current blemishes were little by little being revealed to me. America's sins of slavery, imperialism, and racism were rearing their head in my consciousness. As I replayed in my mind many past conflicts in which America was involved, I noticed that I was sometimes rooting for the other side, for the underdog. In many western movies, the white American cowboys were more villains than heroes and my sympathies lay with the oppressed and dehumanized Indians. Feelings of anguish started lurking below the surface as I tried to reconcile in my mind this dark, evil side of America and my presence in It. Could I be seen as condoning that evil by choosing to be here? I was searching my soul and trying for the first time to make sense of it all.

My then-frequent introspective analyses and the questions it engendered were clearly reflected in "My Ambiguous Adventure," an autobiographical essay I wrote in 1971 for my English 11 course and still carry with me today.

In any case, I continued to run quietly, methodically towards my goal. For the remainder of my college years and throughout medical school, I remained fully aware of my internal turmoil, but I could not, and did not, allow it to shape and determine my every action or decision. I was well aware of issues of discrimination and racism, but somehow I managed to make accommodations in my mind, telling myself that this was only one of the hurdles in my long obstacle course. At the time I saw these issues simply as realities to live with, obstructions to navigate around rather than problems to be solved. Hence, with that right or wrong frame of mind, I did not allow my awareness of these issues to be at the forefront of my daily activities. I could not allow it to hamper my academic pursuits.

I knew, for instance, that if I made a mistake or failed a test, it would be viewed through the lenses of my blackness and my dumb, stupid, inferior, lazy Africanness; whereas if my white colleague did the same, all kinds of excuses and explanations would be found to justify the understanding and compassion accorded to them. While their white privilege allowed for being tired, having distracting family issues, not having enough time to complete a task, and so on, my errors, failures would often be attributed to my innate ineptitude and inferior intellect. So, right or wrong, that became my working assumption in most tasks. I had one chance and one chance only to get it right, since unlike the white students, I would not be given the benefit of the doubt. Furthermore, I refused to use the fact that I was a non-English-speaking foreigner as an excuse or a reason for any of my shortcomings. I worked harder, measured twice and cut once.

This attitude, approach, comportment, served me well during these grueling years, even though there were the occasional, inevitable incidents that required more than tacit acquiescence.

I remember well in my first year at Amherst being deeply offended when I was offered a job as a dishwasher and busboy in the cafeteria. I had no money for personal expenses, no friends or family to rely on. I had no savings and no student loans. I desperately needed a job. But the idea of being offered what I considered then to be a menial job, a servant job, a "slave job," was deeply offensive to me. I was saying to myself, and later out loud, that I was offered these jobs because I was black, because I was African. So, courageously, defiantly, I let it be known to the financial aid officers as well as the admission officers that this was totally unacceptable to me and if they could not provide me a better, more suitable and respectable job, I would rather return home to the Congo. I must have been very persuasive in my argument. I left their offices with a more acceptable and respectable job. I was assigned to the library as a clerk. I stacked returned books or checked out new ones. I also used the ample free time to do my homework or do my own personal reading.

I also remember a brief but deeply revealing incident in my third year in medical school. It was during the clinical rotations. We were then training and interacting with real patients, taking medical history, and performing physical exams. We were also responsible for most of the scut work, including drawing blood and starting intravenous lines for administration of fluids and medications. On one occasion, my chief resident directed me to go to a patient's room. The patient was being "worked up," evaluated for a fever of unknown origin. He was new and unknown to me.

Dressed in my resident white trousers and white jacket, with my toolbox in hand, I entered the patient's room and introduced myself as usual. "Hi, my name is Raphael Tshibangu; I am a medical student. I understand you have a fever and we do not know why. I am sent in to draw some blood from you. We need to do some tests."

"What kind of name is that?" I had heard that kind of question before and did not see the need to answer it. Instead, I smiled and gently approached.

"It will only take a moment," I said as I bent down at his bedside to assess his vein accessibility.

Somewhat to my surprise, he started screaming loudly, "Do not touch me! Do not touch me..., Blackie!" And suddenly, unexpectedly, he spat on my face. Just as fast as he spat, I reflexively slapped him on his right cheek and gave him a stern and combative look. He looked at me incredulously as I picked up my box and left the room to clean my face.

As I recounted what had happened to my chief resident and charge nurse, they tried their best to comfort me. "It was nothing personal," they said. "He is a difficult patient; he has no filter; he is unhappy because he has had many blood draws." Frankly, I did not need their reassurance. Although I may have been slightly shaken, I was actually proud that I had stood my ground. I had defended myself and would not be apologetic for striking this bigot who had so violated me, patient or not.

I would not be intimidated or discouraged. I returned to my scut work. I finished my shift without any further events.

Raphael T. Tshibangu, M.D.

Things Fall Apart

For eight years, I stood my ground. I finished college and graduated from medical school with distinction. I did not set foot in the Congo during this entire time.

To say that I was eager and excited to go back home in 1978, at the conclusion of medical school, would be a huge understatement. The level of anticipation was extremely high, even though I was not entirely sure what I would find there since communication with my family and friends during those eight years was minimal. An occasional postcard or a letter, which sometimes took months to arrive, or an occasional prearranged phone call could not paint a clear picture of what I could expect. Nonetheless, I was yearning to see my family and eager to reconnect with my old friends. I was so impatient to leave that I booked my flight as soon as I found out that I had satisfied all the requirements for my doctorate degree and that my diploma was on its way. I did not want to wait for the graduation ceremony. For me, it was already enough to go back home with a "Doctor" prefix attached to my name. Besides, most of the people that I loved were not able and were not going to be present for such a ceremony, just like they were not able and could not attend my college commencement.

With a few dollars I was able to save from my part-time jobs and student loans (which I was finally able to get in medical school), I managed to stuff two large suitcases with various items, including shoes, pants, suits, blouses, and other articles of clothing, as well as souvenir-type bric-a-bracs, leaving a small corner of one suitcase for my own belongings. Not only did I have to bring gifts after such a long absence, I *wanted* to bring gifts. I wanted to give a good impression. I wanted to please and show that my time away was not squandered. They were expecting it.

I landed at Ndjili Airport in Kinshasa in May 1978 with a mixture of excitement and anticipatory anxiety, uncertain of what lay ahead. Getting off the plane, I was greeted by the thick, warm air emanating from the cracked black tarmac. In front of me was a two-story building in various stages of disrepair. As seen from the broken and uneven tarmac, it looked like a series of rectangular boxes stacked on top of one another in a haphazard fashion. The walls were a dull yellow, the same dull yellow they were eight years prior. There were patches of peeling paint and brownish discoloration, especially where the walls touched the ground. Through the double glass doors was a crowded warehouse-like structure that served as the arrival hall. At the end of the hall were several kiosks in which sat stern and unwelcoming immigration officers ready to pounce, intimidate, and scratch out a bribe whenever they could. Beyond this gauntlet, our luggage was hand delivered, for a small donation, to another cement floored corner of the warehouse. With sadness and annoyance, I watched four or five skinny but vigorous men, "luggage boys," fight over one bag, hustling for a few Congolese francs. As I was picking up my bags and looking for the exit, I was also realizing, with a sinking feeling, that while I had been focused on and running towards my doctorate degree, things back home were falling apart.

Things were falling apart in every respect. Not just in intellectual and cultural ways, as described by Chinua Achebe in his book *Things Fall Apart*, but in very tangible, visible, and palpable ways:

the degrading physical infrastructure due to neglect, the declining socioeconomic development due to failing policies and bankrupt enterprises, the deteriorating mores with the emergence of corruption and victimization, the abuse of good African traditions of community and mutual assistance with the emergence of entitlement and beggary. All these flagrant changes were truly a Mike Tyson–like punch in the face.

No doubt, my soul was appeased after being reconnected with home, albeit briefly. My soul was filled after spending a wonderful time with my family. But at the same it was heavy and saddened at the realization that the "plague" that I was preparing to help eradicate not only had a firm grip on the Congo, but it was worse than when I left nearly a decade prior.

Still determined in my mission, I told and convinced myself that I only had a few more miles to go before my triumphant return. I will return to confront these enormous challenges. I will return to help ease her suffering. I shall be back!

Triumph or Betrayal?

My OB/GYN residency from 1978 to 1982 was a fulfilling time. It was demanding but stimulating and thought provoking. It required the full use of my abilities and most of my time. I had chosen this specialty because I estimated that it would provide me with the necessary medical and surgical skills that I could use upon my return to the Congo where rudimentary conditions still prevailed. Other specialties, such as neurosurgery and cardiothoracic surgery, which were more interesting and intellectually preferable to me, did not appear as practical given the lack of medical infrastructure that could allow for such a practice.

I was pleased with my choice. I could see myself growing and blossoming every year. I was becoming more and more confident in my abilities. I was delighted with the progress in my growth. Soon enough, I went from doctor "Who?" to "Dr. Bango," "Dr. Zhivagho" to "Dr. T" and finally to "Dr. Tshibangu." As a Chief Resident, and even later as an Attending, it gave me slight pleasure when occasionally I would hear a medical student or a new nurse practice the pronunciation of my name before coming to introduce themselves to me. I began to feel like I belonged and was getting closer and closer to my triumph.

And sure enough, the moment I had foreseen fourteen years earlier, at age sixteen, was a reality. At our commencement dinner, like all the previous Chief Residents, I was given a chair as a parting gift. It was an oak wooden chair with a wide, curved, inviting seat and round armrests. It had a golden plaque on the seat back on which is engraved "Dr. Raphael Tshisambu Tshibangu, 1982." I accepted my chair with joy and pride. I looked at and then sat in my chair. At that moment, like Julius Cesar, I felt and silently said, *"Veni, vidi, vinci."* (I came, I saw, I conquered.) I had arrived.

After twenty years of schooling, I was finally a proud American-trained obstetrician-gynecologist. Not arrogant, loud, or flamboyant, but quietly confident, self-assured of my ability to practice competently anywhere in the world.

I would experience the same sense of pride in my achievement about two years later when I became inducted as a Fellow of the American College of Obstetricians and Gynecologists. Not a small feat, considering how grueling the admission process is.

Raphael T. Tshibangu, M.D.

Induction into the fellowship, which is partly a confirmation of competence and partly a hazing ritual, begins with a written exam that is taken at some specified dates after completion of the residency. One is then given a minimum of two years to adjust to private practice and to compile a case list comprising every single surgical procedure, patient hospitalization, delivery, and office visit. Once the case list is accepted, the candidate can schedule an oral exam: The Oral Boards. Many young physicians usually do so after spending thousands of dollars on preparatory courses offered around the country. Like many fellows, I can still vividly remember travelling to Chicago that cold November day in 1983 and registering for the boards in the hotel where the oral exams were given. The hotel was taken over by a crowd of anxious overachievers nervously fidgeting through pages of *Williams Obstetrics*, Leon Speroff's *Clinical Gynecologic Endocrinology and Infertility*, and other major textbooks. These highly educated professionals were forgoing their meals and were silently begging for more time to cram in the last bit of knowledge. They were in the hallways, in the lobby, in the coffee shop, clearly frightened and barely looking up to acknowledge passersby, let alone to say hello.

The air was thick with the palpable fear of failure, which historically claimed on the average one in six candidates. And even though the results were not widely published, we all knew that our colleagues and interested institutions would eventually find out. So, the thought of being one the failing candidates and facing the likelihood of repeating this process was unfathomable. Everybody was understandably stressed because we all understood the gravity of this moment. Everybody, that is, except for the Distinguished Professors who seemed to relish the sight of the squirming lambs who voluntarily offered themselves for a barbecue. Surely, these mostly white, male master teachers needed us to demonstrate clinical competence in the care of patients; and to that end, they probed, pushed, asked whys and hows until the candidate could no longer answer the barrage of questions and admitted defeat. At which point the candidate could never be entirely certain if they had passed or failed and could only surmise their fate by scrutinizing the faces of the ferocious examiners.

Having been previously briefed about this ritual, I had planned to check into an adjacent hotel to remove myself from these anxiety-laden scenes. I took refuge in my room and pretended to read. I ordered room service but hardly ate for lack of appetite. My mind was unsettled and racing; I could not sleep. The following day, a very long day, I endured the expected hazing and hurriedly took my flight back home that evening. Did I pass? Did I fail? What excuse can I conjure up to explain a possible eventual rejection?

I remained somewhat numb during the flight, exhausted but unable to rest.

When I arrived home, I was greeted with a congratulatory kiss from Sherry. I was somewhat puzzled, but I obliged, thinking that she was just being supportive and was congratulating me for my effort. Little did I know that Dr. Georges Trombetta, who was Chief of my department at Highland, as well as a board examiner, had called home and informed her that I had passed the exam. He must have known how agonizing it was to wait for that dreaded letter containing the results to come in several days later.

I was immensely relieved. Another battle was won. Another mark of distinction.

A few months later, at the induction ceremony, I felt triumphant as I put on the dark green gown and cap, and was conferred the honor, privileges, and responsibilities of a Fellow of the American College of Ob-Gyn. And to commemorate the occasion, Sherry and I had a portrait of this joyful occasion made.

Alas, my feelings of triumph were short lived. They were somewhat muted, maybe because I could not share them with any of my family. They may also have been subdued because deep down I knew this moment would come and when it finally arrived it was anticlimactic. Maybe, and most likely, it was because of the uncertainty of what lay ahead.

What now?

I knew from my previous research that there were only a few possible employers in the Congo at the time. They included the once-mighty Gécamines; the national railroad company, SNCZ; the university clinics. I could certainly get a job at any of them. I was qualified—*more* than qualified! I could at least start there until I get my feet wet and figure out the best way forward.

Unfortunately, as I started my inquiries, I was startled at how far things had continued to fall apart compared to a mere four years earlier when I had a chance to visit. The downward spiral was dizzying: hospital equipment no longer updated; empty shelves in hospital pharmacies; inpatient families had to bring in their own medications, surgical instruments, and food for their loved ones. Hospitals had become the place where people were going to die. Those who had the means were leaving the country for appropriate care. Many of the employed physicians and professionals were poorly paid and sometimes worked for months without pay. Many had already left the country for South Africa, Zambia, Gabon, and many more were looking desperately for a way out.

It was unthinkable and unimaginable that a mass exodus of professionals was under way considering the huge and urgent need for healthcare workers.

I contacted a few private clinics. Most, even the ones that expressed some interest if a position became available, required my presence for a face-to-face interview. No positions immediately available. No guarantees of any openings in the near future. Unthinkable!

In addition, a practice license for the Congo was required, understandably, but would take at a minimum several months and, as I sadly found out, could take up to two years.

Impossible! I did not have the resources to open my own clinic or wait around for the time it would take to get the license. What now? The obstacles were clearly mounting. They were accumulating beyond anything I could have predicted or even imagined. All my friends, without exception—my eyes and ears on the ground—unequivocally advised me not to come back. Incredulous at the beginning, they finally convinced me when they privately confided in me that many of them were also looking for a way out.

During these agonizing days, weeks, and months, I already had a job that was offered to me, unsolicited, upon my graduation. Furthermore, by this time, I had been married for more than two years; I felt a sense of responsibility. So, I listened, somewhat reluctantly, to my friends and family who encouraged me to stay. They did not want me to return, at least not then. I heeded their advice. I told myself, "Maybe I will go back later." Unbelievable outcome! I took the job.

There was now a fissure in my previously solid conviction and foundation. To go back or not to go back was never a question. But there I was, accepting and starting a job I was not looking for. I had decided to stay in America and I was telling myself and others, not always convincingly, that I had no choice.

I diligently performed my duties as a new Attending at Highland Hospital, a Clinical Instructor for the University of Rochester and as an employee of the Rochester Medical Group. But every now and then I would still wonder, "Did I really have no choice? Did I do the right thing?"

In 1984, another trip to Zaire exposed the widening fissure in my "Rieux" foundation even more. Everything I had seen and experienced in 1978 was a thousand times worse. The already old infrastructure was crumbling and disintegrating at warp speed. Corruption was rampant and had permeated every level of government, business, and civil society. Police harassment at every street corner made travel inside the country a hellish adventure. I remember one such adventurous day. Funny today, but somewhat reckless in retrospect.

It was a couple of days after we arrived in Lubumbashi. My sister-in-law Charlotte, Sherry, and I decided to go for a sightseeing tour around the city before going on to Likasi to visit my brother Alphonse and his family. It was a beautiful, mildly warm, and sunny day. My brother Vincent, who could not come with us because of his work schedule, encouraged us to do so and put his relatively new Peugeot at our disposal. Being aware of all the "customary" traffic stops when driving around town, he diligently made sure that the car was in perfect order, with registration and insurance

*A crowning achievement indeed, but
only a rung on the ladder of life, 1984.*

papers, spare tire, and hazard triangle sign—all the things that the police would often ask for. As we left the house, I also made sure that we had all our identification papers, including passports and international driving license. As soon as we reached downtown, it did not take long before we encountered the first of many inspection stops. There were no particular reasons given for these traffic checks. We were all well aware that these were simply occasions for the underpaid traffic cops and military police to make some money. Often working in bunches, they would walk and circle around the car looking for possible infractions. They often asked for the usual papers, which they did not even look, at but would often hold on to before the negotiations began. They would almost never ask for money upfront, but it was understood that payment was the only ticket out of this harassment. And if a driver was not fully aware of what they were requesting they would sometimes say, "I am thirsty, how about a *simba* (beer)?" or "My child needs milk," a more respectable request. So, since I did not have the time nor the inclination to engage in such a pestering and frustrating game, I would quickly brandish the equivalent of a $10 or $20 bill in Zairean currency (Zaires/Makuta), which they quickly snatched out of my hand and just as quickly tucked into their pockets. They would then gleefully clear the way, give a military salute, and wish us a blessed day as they cleared the way for our car.

Each time, Sherry would admonish me for giving in so quickly and contributing to this culture of corruption. My response was that we had to be realistic and pragmatic; we did not have all day to argue with these starving, desperate but determined so-called cops. This was not the time for a civics lesson. So we went on and I kept paying. Until I, too, became exasperated.

As we were leaving town on our way to Likasi, there was one more barrier right at the edge of town. It was simply made of a long piece of wood supported by two large metal bins. On the side of the road were half a dozen emaciated individuals in military fatigues. Sitting on tree trunks, with long guns at their side, they seemed to be tending the barrier. As we approached, I slowed down the car and allowed them to slowly remove the piece of wood that was lying across the metal bins. Two or three of them were going around the car in their usual inspection ritual, circling prey before moving in for the kill. Without any forethought, I stepped on the accelerator as I impulsively decided to make a run for it. Through the roar of the car engine we could hear menacing commands of *"Arretez! Arretez…"* ("Stop! Stop…") but it was too late to change my mind and all I could do is ask my sister-in-law and my wife to get down as I quickly took a peak in the rear view mirror at the surprised officers who were suddenly, unexpectedly, left brandishing their guns in our direction. Were the guns loaded or not? I did not know. I do not know.

A few minutes later we were able to finally catch our breath as we realized that they had no way of coming after us since they did not have any vehicles. Our palpitations subsided, and with the heart rate back to normal, we spent several minutes laughing about the incident. In retrospect, I thought, it would have been better to pay the *Makuta* "toll."

Many more incidents would follow in our interactions with the police and government officials. Sometimes funny but mostly infuriating, discouraging, and depressing.

Citizenship

Despite the many incidents of intimidation, badgering, and extortion, we made the best of our trip as I reconnected again with my family, and Sherry finally met my parents.

However, these observations, as well as my upcoming humiliating experiences at the Brussels airport, would become pivotal in my metamorphosis.

Raphael T. Tshibangu, M.D.

Our return itinerary included an overnight transit in Brussels. We had already booked a hotel room expecting to spend a restful night prior to our connection flight to New York. Upon arrival at the airport, Congolese/Zairean citizens were separated from the rest of the passengers for a particularly thorough inspection. Like presumed criminals, we were led to a long, narrow corridor that led to two small interrogation rooms. The corridor was dark, damp, and the air was thick with a combination of moldy smells and body odors. A cement wall stood on one side and thick clear glass on the other. Through the glass door I could see my wife and other passengers going through inspection quickly and effortlessly. They appeared to be treated with dignity. On our side, we looked like cattle slowly being herded to slaughter. After a few of hours—which seemed like an eternity—it was my turn to be interviewed: "What is your full name? Where did you get the passport? How long have you been in the U.S.? What do you do in the U.S.? How long are you going to be in the U.S.? Do you have your marriage certificate? Why do you want to spend the night in Brussels?" And so it went on with a thousand more stupid, intrusive, and annoying questions. For some unclear reason, the transit visa I had used on my way down was no longer valid. I would have to spend the night at the airport in their detention area until the next day. It was a bare waiting area with several benches and a couple of bathrooms. There was no access to the airport lounges or restaurants and there were no amenities. Mostly black, tired, and sad faces filled the area, each with their own stories. It was truly incredible to see the disrespect and callousness that some of my compatriots and I were subjected to. Presumed criminal or just undesirable, simply for being Zairean.

Long after the interrogation, we continued to plead our case, I on the inside and Sherry on the "free" side. Finally, the officers were able to confirm to their satisfaction the validity of our documents and were also able to confirm that we had indeed made a reservation at a well-known hotel for a single night. Hours after the ordeal began, we were ultimately allowed to leave the airport. We managed to rest for a few hours and catch our return flight to New York without any further escapades.

As I relived those previous days, I realized that I must have been profoundly affected by all those events. I was starting to question my ability and my willingness to affect any meaningful changes in Zaire. I saw myself as a tiny midget standing at the gates of Hell, thinking about how to put out the Fire. What was the point? I thought about Brussels and asked myself, "What is the point of carrying a Zairean passport? Why not get a U.S. passport?"

Why not become a U.S. citizen?

After all, many of my friends and family members were referring to me as "the American." They had assumed or perceived, long before I had any conscious realization, that many of my values, aspirations, and wishes had become more and more aligned with American values. Indeed, I espoused the ideas of democracy, individual freedom and justice, self-reliance, and hard work. I believed and still do that hard work should be rewarded by material wealth. I believed equality in the rights—as well responsibilities—of citizens. And I believed in equal opportunity. So, why not become a U.S. citizen?

I did not fully ponder or answer that question to my satisfaction. I was so dejected and disgusted by my recent experiences that soon after we returned to Rochester, I applied for U.S. citizenship.

I applied for an American passport at the same time. I wanted no more hassles, no more disrespect. I wanted to be able to travel more easily and freely, in and out of the United States. I wanted a *real* passport.

And so, several months later when I became a U.S. citizen, it was not only because I longed for and wanted to fully, exclusively, embrace all the "American values," which were certainly not the monopoly of America. It was also and mainly for pragmatic reasons. An American passport is respected. An American passport gives you access to most countries without the need for a visa. I was happy and felt privileged to carry one.

However, the naturalization ceremony was not a big deal for me. It was not a big affair. There was no celebration, no fanfare, no flag waving. At the courthouse, where a few newly minted citizen assembled for the usually festive and momentous ceremony, it was just my wife, myself, and a good dose of ambivalence. Ambivalent because I was happy to become an American with all the rights, privileges, and responsibilities. But I also felt a sense of loss and betrayal since the Pledge of Allegiance called for renouncing my Congolese citizenship. I may have uttered those words then, but I am sure I did not mean to.

Fortunately, whatever twinges of betrayal I was harboring dissipated rather quickly. I realized that my heart and soul had not betrayed my homeland or my family. I firmly believed that despite the unpredicted course of events and the disappointments, my attachment to Home and Family was still strong. It had not evaporated because of this pledge. My pledge of renunciation was on paper only. Deep inside I am and will stay Congolese.

I remembered at that time a poem that I had read several years prior. It was the early '70s. The inspiring words were written on an adorned parchment used as a placemat at a Howard Johnson's restaurant in Cambridge, Massachusetts. "Desiderata" is the title of the poem, which I had kept in my possession all those years. I read it again. I also listened to different recordings that I had become aware of since that first reading. I listened again and again. Those words spoke to me, inspired me, and gave me a sense of peace as I proceeded in my new quest for the American Dream as a naturalized American citizen.

Written by Max Ehrmann (1872–1945), a child of German immigrants, and recorded by Les Crane in 1971, this beautiful poem about life is worth reproducing in its entirety.

> Desiderata. Desiderata. Desiderata.
> Go placidly amid the noise and haste,
> And remember what peace there may be in silence.
> As far as possible, without surrender,
> Be in good terms with all persons.
> Speak your truth quietly and clearly; and listen to others,
> Even the dull and ignorant; they too have their story.
> Avoid loud and aggressive; they are vexations to the spirit.
> If you compare yourself with others, you may become vain and bitter,
> For always there will be greater and lesser persons than you.
> Enjoy your achievements as well as your plans.

Raphael T. Tshibangu, M.D.

Keep interested in your own career,
However humble, it is a real possession in the changing fortunes of time.
Exercise caution in your business affairs, for the world is full of trickery.
But let this not blind you to what virtue there is;
Many persons strive for high ideals, and everywhere life is full of heroism.
Be yourself.
Especially do not feign affection, neither be cynical about love;
For in the face of all aridity and disenchantment,
It is as perennial as the grass.
Take kindly the counsel of the years,
Gracefully surrendering the things of youth.
Nurture strength of spirit to shield you in sudden misfortune.
But do not distress yourself with imaginings.
Many fears are born of fatigue and loneliness.
Beyond a wholesome discipline, be gentle with yourself.
You are a child of the universe
No less than the trees and the stars; you have a right to be here.
And whether or not it is clear to you.
No doubt the universe is unfolding as it should.

> Therefore, be at peace with God, whatever you conceive Him to be.
> And whatever your labors and aspirations, in the noisy confusion of life,
> Keep peace with your soul.
> With all its sham, drudgery and broken dreams, it is still a beautiful world.
> Be careful. Strive to be happy.

The Universe was unfolding.

With the changing fortunes and misfortunes of time, I saw my dream of becoming Dr. Rieux crumbling. I did not go back when I had hope, and it was becoming clear to me that I may not. At least, not anytime soon. So it was that in the late '80s and most of the '90s I went placidly amid the noise and haste, slowly but gradually building my American Dream.

My career was challenging and exhilarating. I was full of energy then. Often working 80 to 120 hours a week. I would often put in a full day in the office after only a couple of hours of sleep. I had the kind of energy that allowed me to deliver up to 200 patients a year. I did so for many years.

On one occasion in particular I even felt like Superman. I was not on call that night and was sleeping soundly in my warm bed. The house phone, which was always next to my ear, rang and I picked it up before the first ring was over. It was about 3:00 a.m. "Dr. B. is in the O.R. and he needs you," said a nurse's voice at the end of the line. Although she was calm and composed, her terse message conveyed a sense of a dire emergency and no questions needed to be asked. I was gargling a mouthwash while getting dressed and walking to my car in the garage at the same time. While in the car I was trying to imagine what kind of emergency I would be dealing with, but nothing specific came to mind. Possible diagnoses and scenarios were twirling in my mind. I did not have enough time to focus on any. I was already parking my car, illegally, in front of the hospital and rushing up the staircase to the second floor where the labor and delivery O.R.s were located. Before I knew it, I was walking in the O.R., donning my scrubs and a surgical mask as soapy water was dripping from my elbows, following an abbreviated scrub. Eyes wide open, I was focusing on the operating field as I was being briefed. The patient had had an emergency C-section due to a placental abruption. The baby was doing well but the mother was experiencing an uncontrollable postpartum hemorrhage. She had been bleeding profusely despite vigorous massage and administration of different oxytocics. There was blood everywhere on the operating field and even on the O.R. floor next to the operating table. The anesthesiologist assured me that the patient was stable. She had already received four pints of blood and there were four more on the way. I gently nudged the assisting resident aside. We calmly assessed the situation and decided on a procedure that would save the patient's uterus rather than doing a faster and more predictable hysterectomy. With composure, we performed a B-Lynch suture and a uterine artery ligation while continuing oxytocics administration. We managed to control the bleeding while sparing the patient's uterus and her capacity for future reproduction.

With a great feeling of relief, we closed the patient's abdomen and transported her to the recovery room in stable condition.

And, as I was sitting in the nurse's station, sipping a cup of tea, which was my customary reward following a satisfactory outcome intervention, we all wondered how I was able to be in the O.R. so fast! Some wondered whether I was already in the hospital, even though they knew I was called on my house phone. In fifteen minutes, I was able to get up, get dressed, drive the usual twenty-minute distance to the hospital, change in my scrubs and take control of a challenging operation. Well, I do not know how, but I know it happened so. It was a Superman moment.

Many more moments of satisfaction would follow. I always enjoyed watching the amazing transformation from a high anxiety and painful labor course to a beautiful joyful moment once the baby was delivered and safely in the mother's hands; emotionally connecting, skin to skin. Each birth was miraculous. Most were easy to attend to and some were complex and complicated, requiring skillful interventions to safeguard the health of the mother and the baby. These stressful, sometimes unexpected situations were also usually more rewarding when, in the end, the outcome was favorable.

I particularly remember of one of the first patients with shoulder dystocia that I managed.

Shoulder dystocia is an obstetric emergency that is often unexpectedly diagnosed when the normal traction on the baby's head does not lead to the delivery of the shoulders. The shoulders are stuck above the mother's pubic bone and this is manifested by the delivered-baby's head appearing to be retracting back in the vagina. This "turtle" sign is an alarm bell that requires swift action to prevent possible harm to the baby, including brain injury due to a lack of oxygen, damage to the spinal cord nerves in the neck area that can result in permanent paralysis, and fracture of the arms and/or clavicles.

My patient had had an uneventful prenatal course. The estimated fetal weight was around eight pounds. Her labor course was also normal, unremarkable. After pushing for about an hour and a half, the head was delivered. Then: a quick snap back, an obvious turtle sign, a rush of adrenaline.

I remained composed and called for immediate assistance as I engaged the McRoberts maneuver. With maternal hips flexed and wide open, suprapubic pressure was applied to dislodge the shoulders while gentle rotation was simultaneously performed. An episiotomy was made to enlarge the opening as I also tried to manually deliver the posterior shoulder first. Finally, after what seemed like an eternity, there was a click sound as the shoulders and the rest of the baby was delivered.

There was a huge sigh of relief when, a minute or so later, the baby, who was being attended to by the pediatricians previously called in for this emergency, started crying. What a sweet sound!

More relaxed, we turned our attention to the mother, controlled the bleeding, stitched, and cleaned.

Once outside the delivery room, the pediatrician informed me that the baby had sustained a fracture of the clavicle, which is not an uncommon occurrence under these circumstances and usually heals very well without any major interventions. Still, I was somewhat distraught as I went on to attend to other patients.

Later that day, when I return to the patient's room to explain to her what had happened and reassure her about the fracture, I was greeted with profuse thank-yous. "I know what happened," she said. "I was so scared when I saw all those doctors and nurses come running in. I thought my baby was going to die. They told me that you did a great Job. Thank you for saving my baby." I was flabbergasted. I thought I was coming in to apologize about the fracture, reassure the patient that the baby prognosis was excellent, but instead she was consoling me, congratulating me for a job well done! It was a very satisfying day indeed.

I am also recurrently reminded of a patient who, for the past thirty-some years, thanks me every time she sees me, for saving her baby. SK was a young twenty-four-year-old when I first met her. Even though she was in excellent health, she was often concerned about her fertility, as she always expressed her desire to have a big family. She had five siblings and she wanted at least four children.

When she became pregnant about three years later, she was understandably ecstatic—extremely ecstatic. Unfortunately, her joy quickly faded only a few weeks later when she developed severe nausea and vomiting. Her hyperemesis gravidarum, as it is called, was so severe that she required dozens of hospital trips for intravenous hydration, electrolytes, and vitamin supplements. Unlike most cases of hyperemesis, which tend to improve in the second trimester, hers persisted and seemed to worsen. No approved antiemetics were helpful; she was losing an unhealthy amount of weight and was bedridden most of the day. She desperately wanted this pregnancy and would do whatever was required. But she, or I, could not have imagined how truly miserable she would get. At about fifteen weeks of gestation, her husband literally carried her to my office for a consultation. He explained, "We have thought about it; we have prayed about it. Her health is in danger. We want an abortion." I was not surprised at the request and actually anticipated it when they made this urgent appointment. Knowing what SK had already told me about wanting a large family, I was also determined to help her keep at least this one.

I knew, and I so informed them, about an antipsychotic medication, Haldol, that had been shown to be quite effective in severe cases of nausea experienced by many cancer patients on chemotherapy. It certainly was not approved for use in pregnancy and clearly the long-term side effects on the fetus/baby were unknown.

So, I suggested that we admit SK to the hospital for hyperalimentation-intravenous feeding and start her on Haldol treatment. And if this fails as well, I assured them, I would arrange for her to undergo a pregnancy termination. SK managed to faintly nod yes, and her husband reluctantly agreed.

After a week or so, SK was back home. She was able to tolerate small amounts of food and had put on weight. She continued to experience occasional bouts of nausea and vomiting, but nothing remotely resembling the previous weeks. Although she felt somewhat sleepy and lethargic because of the medication, and although she continued to travel with a dull, greyish tin spit bucket and a washcloth for the remainder of her pregnancy, we were all glad that we had managed to avert a dreadful decision.

In the back of my mind, however, I kept wondering how the hyperemesis gravidarum and all the treatments we used—including and especially Haldol—were going to affect the development of the fetus and the baby. With fewer fetal monitoring tools available to us then, I anxiously held my breath and hoped for the best. Needless to say, it was quite a relief when SK made it to term and delivered a slightly over six-pound baby with all its fingers and its toes. The Apgar score, measuring the newborn's health, of 9 out of 10 was exhilarating.

From that day on, every time I saw SK, she would thank me for saving her baby. "I tell everybody how you saved my baby," she would often say as she gave me an update, which was always good and reassuring for me. And I could not be more satisfied when recently, thirty-four years after that AB Consult (abortion consultation) she told me that her son is a board-certified neurosurgeon, practicing at one of the prestigious hospitals in the country.

I enjoyed doing surgery as well. Some of my colleagues complimented me by asking me to lend a hand during difficult cases and often made reference to my "magic hand." I was truly enjoying my career as I progressed from Instructor to Assistant Professor and Associate Professor of OB/GYN at the University of Rochester. I was Board Certified and a Fellow of the American College of OB/GYN.

In my clinical practice, the stars were also aligned. I became chief of the OB/GYN department of the Rochester Medical Group in 1986 and continued in that role until 1991. Subsequently, one of my colleagues, Dr. Eufemia Mariano, and I decided to venture out on our own and started a private practice in May 1991. Southeast OB/GYN, as it was called, is still thriving as I write. We presently have four physicians, two Nurse Practitioners, and many staff, some who have been with me from opening day.

At the same time and despite the busy and exhausting 80 to 120 hours per week of medical practice, life outside of work went on as well. Flourishing in many aspects, it inevitably had moments of disappointment and anguish. Our Rochester family was slowly but gradually growing. Four years after our marriage, having accepted my inability to have any children, we adopted our daughter, Titi. A few years later, in 1987, my younger brother Albert, who had left Rochester to pursue his MBA in California, came back to rejoin us. His wife, Odette, and their two U.S.-born children, ChiChi and Channy, would constitute our nuclear family in America for a while. Later, the family was extended further with the arrival of three of my nephews (Albert, Ting, Douglas) and the addition of their own children. There would be a few more nephews and nieces, and as time went on, more and more grand-nephews and -nieces.

It seemed then that I could not ask for more. I had a thriving career, a growing extended family, a brick house in the suburbs, luxury foreign cars, multiple yearly vacations over land and sea. I had all the appearances of living the American Dream.

Ambivalence

But, as my roots grew deeper and stronger in America, my roots in the Congo were becoming dehydrated, emaciated, and flimsy.

The deaths of my father in 1995, my mother in 1998, my older brother/cousin Barthelemy, my best friend, Cele, in 2000, and of many others in quick succession during the same time frame were each and cumulatively more and more devastating to my psyche. I am not certain, but I believe now that these events, in addition to the overall political and socioeconomic conditions in the country, were a major catalyst in my subconscious metamorphosis. I became less and less interested in the Congo. I was less hopeful about the prospects of a better life in the Congo and started to believe that the Congo would not amount to anything for at least another hundred years. I, as well as some of my friends, felt defeated by these devastating events and tried to find some refuge in laughter, as we could not avoid witnessing the Congolese tragicomedy. We took solace in our ability to breathe some life into a few countrymen and family members by sending money through Western Union or MoneyGram.

Hope had turned into despair and concern into cynicism. Instead of brainstorming about what we could do to help, as we often did, we started to joke about the conditions in the Congo. One such, encapsulating, joke was widely circulated: Reagan, Mitterrand, Thatcher, and Mobutu were taking a break from their daily chores in hell. Curious about how their compatriots were doing in their respective countries, they decided to call and check in. A nearby payphone was available and fiercely guarded by one of Lucifer's disciples. Reagan was first. He called Washington, D.C., and talked for about a minute. He was beaming with joy and pride as he was reassured that America was still the only superpower and that all has been well since the fall of the Berlin Wall. The guard sternly approached and demanded $10,000,000 for the phone call, which Reagan paid begrudgingly. Mitterrand was second. A quick call to the Champs-Élysées, he too was reassured that France was still in great shape. France was still master of the CFA (*Communauté Financière d'Afrique*) and still successfully promoting *La Francophonie*. After one minute, the guard yelled, "One million dollars!" He gladly paid, noting that it was less than what his friend Reagan had just paid.

Raphael T. Tshibangu, M.D.

Thatcher was next. London was busy planning the Olympic games. More and more people around the world are speaking English and taking a liking to fish and chips. "One million dollars," the guard declared about a minute later. Thatcher was also happy to pay, remarking that the U.K. was on par with France and she did not have to pay any less or any more. Lastly, Mobutu took the phone and called Kinshasa. He talked for over an hour and still could not get through the long list of grievances and lamentations. Since it was the end of the break, the guard slowly approached the payphone. He somberly removed the phone from Mobutu's blood-stained hands and said, "No charge." As they heard "no charge," Reagan, Mitterrand, and Thatcher became suddenly infuriated and demanded an explanation. How is it that we paid millions of dollars for a one-minute call and this guy pays nothing for a one-hour call. The guard turned his head towards them, shaking it slightly from side to side, and matter-of-factly responded, "You stupid imperialist morons, don't you realize that yours were long-distance calls and his is a local call." Such moments of levity multiplied. We had to laugh to keep from crying. Our conversations were always based in reality, but often laced with a good dose of cynicism and protective detachment.

I had personally experienced, more like witnessed, albeit for brief moments, these hellish realities as I travelled to the Congo in 1995, '98, 2000, '06, '08, '12, and '16.

At the same time, unintentionally, unconsciously, I was inadvertently becoming more and more American and struggling to remain Congolese. I noticed a change in nuance when I answered the question "Where are you from?"

"I am from Rochester, New York," I would say.

"Yeah, but where are you from? Where were you born? Your accent, your look…"

"I am originally from the Congo," I would add succinctly and sometimes elaborating if I noticed a genuine interest on the part of the questioner.

I was no longer offended. I was no longer annoyed that people wanted to know where I came from and I was not ashamed to let them know. Without reproach and without excuses. Just a simple statement of fact.

Occasionally, if one was interested, I would briefly, dispassionately, and without judgement, describe the course of my journey. There were no more explanations needed. After all, I am a child of the Universe, no less than the trees and the stars. I have a right to be here just like I had the right to be there.

Giving Back. Making a Difference?

I became more and more appreciative of the opportunities that America, and many others in the Congo, had provided me. A scholarship to an elite boarding school in the Congo; admission to a top-tier college in the U.S. with free room and board; a world-class medical school and residency program; a job that gave me nearly unlimited opportunities to go freely around the world and allowed me to assist my family in the Congo more so, I would like to believe, than if I had gone back.

Indeed, even though at the time it was unclear to me, I was realizing that the Universe was unfolding as it should. And as so stated in "Desiderata," I consciously decided to go placidly amid the noise and haste, comfortably navigating the changing fortunes of life. I spoke my truths clearly and quietly. I enjoyed my career in which I still found meaning and satisfaction. I tried to find inspiration by listening to others such as Wayne Dyer, a prolific author and motivational speaker who showed me—*convinced* me—that no amount of feeling bad is ever going to change a painful situation. Indeed, no amount of feeling sad, angry, disappointed, worried is going to change evil into good. Action is always required. Action, whenever possible and however small, is always preferrable.

So, instead of dwelling on, complaining, and whining about the harsh realities in the Congo—instead of ignoring them and hiding behind cynicism, with the constant encouragement from my wife—I started again to think about multiple ways of affecting positive change whenever and wherever possible.

Like many other African immigrants, and Congolese immigrants in particular, I kept sending cash back home through friends, banks, and, most frequently, through wire services. Thousands and thousands of dollars at the exorbitant fees of six to ten percent went home through the wires of Western Union and MoneyGram.

I also tried my hand at multiple investment projects in the Congo.

I tried agriculture. It looked like a no-brainer. The land is vast and fertile. The need insatiable. Our grandfathers and those before them depended solely on it and survived. Why not agriculture? It should be obvious to any observer. We should not go hungry with such an abundant variety of food crops that can be easily cultivated. We should not need to import any foods or food products. With that in mind, agriculture became one of my first projects in the Congo. My brother Vincent, with my financial assistance, cultivated large fields of manioc, maize, and peanuts near my mother's village of Bakodila, Bena Mpoyi in Kasai. My uncle Kabongo, mother's younger brother, was the local manager. He had a lot of energy and he put his heart and soul in the project. As the work progressed, we felt like we had made a great decision; we felt proud that we were able to do something to help our own people.

Unfortunately, the initial enthusiasm was quickly crushed. As this morbid medical joke goes, "The operation was successful, but the patient died." The abundant crops were either consumed for free by extended family members (i.e., the entire clan) or left to rot on the ground because it could not reach the market due to poor infrastructure. Despite my uncle's and my brother's valiant efforts, this once-promising venture was abandoned three short years later. Our good intentions were no match for the challenges we ultimately faced.

I tried transportation.

I purchased a minibus slated to be used for public transportation and a large truck to be used for transporting cargo. Here too, there was no question about the need for such services. In my mind, this venture, if successful, would be a sure moneymaker because it would provide a much-needed service. It would provide some employment and certainly a source of income for my family. I had seen others start from such small beginnings and achieve great things.

Alas, this time, mismanagement issues and frequent equipment failure for which there were no immediately available replacement parts crippled and bankrupted the venture. After a promising beginning, it was time to move on barely two years later.

I tried commerce.

It has been mostly small-scale: tiny boutiques or market kiosks where most of my sisters tried their hand. Different ventures included a pharmacy, a *buvette* (bar-restaurant-café), a clothing boutique, and even diamond trading. These efforts have gone on for several years and with different family members. Here, too, bankruptcy has been the end result, either due to inexperience, lack of know-how, mismanagement, bad luck, or all of the above.

I also tried real estate.

Partnering with friends, we have invested in a few single homes as well as apartment buildings, with relatively modest success. A ray of hope? Maybe?

It should also be pointed out that our efforts to give back, to assist others has not been limited to immediate family members. Fully cognizant of all the help we have received along the way from many strangers, my wife, daughter, and I started RTST Foundation in 2001 with the humble vision of restoring health, touching hearts, shaping the future, and transforming lives. As spelled out in the Foundation mission, we have donated equipment and medicines to small clinics, provided school supplies, awarded some scholarships, and have continued to do so, although not as passionately in recent years.

To further these efforts, in 2008, we also started a for-profit company, TransContinental Commerce (TCC). It was a major foray in social entrepreneurship, a challenging undertaking, with the objective of providing lightly used articles of clothing at reduced prices and using the proceeds to fund our RTST mission. The venture was started with a lot of promise and performed according to expectations for several years. We provided employment to many, especially newly arriving refugees from the DRC and other African countries; we shipped affordable clothing to many African countries but mostly to the Congo; we raised some money for the Foundation. All was going according to plan until many predictable and unpredictable roadblocks reared their head. The escalating fuel and transportation costs, the sudden and unreasonable increases in customs fees and tariffs, and the rampant corruption in the Congo finally forced us to close our doors about four years later. Today, there remains hardly any visible signs of these efforts. All the help we provided seemed to have amounted to a small drop of water in a bottomless bucket.

Misery and suffering continue to reign at a scale so far greater than any help we could provide. With passing time, sadly, many Congolese, including those in my family, have fatalistically adopted a profoundly disconcerting poverty mentality and comportment that has inevitably led to resignation, laziness, surrender, constant begging, corruption, jealousy, and prostitution. Even small children have adopted the saying, "If you do not ask you will not receive." Many have also found refuge in religion and in the exploitative, ever-present mini- and megachurches that have continued to sprout at every street corner, in every town and village. These churches have devious, hypocritical, and profiteering pastors who are more con artists preying on the weak, poor, and unsuspecting rather than true men of God who should be inspiring, motivating, praying for, and consoling their followers.

Conundrum!

One may understandably ask: Why continue to try after so many failures? Why continue to send money and thus enable nonenterprising behavior? Why continue to send donations, such as medical equipment and supplies, when some, if not most, is being diverted for personal use by underpaid and often unpaid hospital employees? Why continue to start businesses in an environment with poor infrastructure and rampant corruption? Is it guilt, family obligation, social obligation, sense of responsibility, all of the above? I may not know for sure. What I do know is that as I continue to strive and find my rightful happy place in this Universe, I will have to deal with what Nigerian author Chimamanda Ngozi Adichie calls "The Thing Around Your Neck." Always present, even though dormant but just below the surface; That Thing around the neck, always tugging and occasionally, agonizingly tightening the noose.

Changing Times?

In December 2018, Félix Tshiombo Tshisekedi won the presidential elections in the DRC. Despite the devious maneuvers, self-interested machinations of Western countries to install their own puppet, Martin Fayulu, Tshisekedi was inaugurated on January 24, 2019. It was a peaceful transition of power, the first in the Congo since its independence in June 1960. Fatshi, as he is affectionately called, is the son of Étienne Tshisekedi, the legendary nationalist opposition leader who fought relentlessly for more than thirty years to restore democracy and establish a nation of law and order.

Fatshi, many hoped, would finally—and befittingly—have a chance to bring his father's work to fruition.

Law and order, the end of corruption, economic development—those were his refrain during his campaign. "People first" was his slogan and his father's for many years. "Let us build it together" was his call to arms for all the willing Congolese people in the country and the Diaspora. Let's build it together was also his plea to the neighboring countries who had contributed to the destruction of the DRC and to all the countries interested in the immense resources of the DRC. To all who would listen, he proposed cooperation and equity in the exploration, production, and enjoyment of the much envied and needed riches of the DRC. "*Un partenariat gagnant-gagnant*," he would often say. ("A win-win partnership.") That was his appeal to foreign governments and foreign investors. The hope he brought to most Congolese was palpable. Many of us were hopeful that this time it will be different, that this time it will be better. Hopeful and yet fearful that, as in the past, the disappointment could be just around the corner.

I had a chance to bask in that renewed hope, enthusiasm, and energy when, in April 2019 I had a chance to meet the new president on his first presidential visit to the United States. His warmth, charisma, sincerity, and determination to fulfill his campaign promises and his father's dream were evident as he addressed some of us in a small lunch meeting at the Mayflower Hotel in Washington, D.C.— the same Mayflower Hotel where I celebrated Independence Day with our embassy staff fifty years earlier. Thousands of Congolese, young and old, traveled from distant parts of the United States and Canada to hear personally the same message of hope and renewal. As we congregated in small groups before and after his meetings, as well as for the First Lady's intimate address to the Congolese *mamans* (mothers), many of us started asking again, "What can we do? What should we do for the Congo?" We talked a lot about Those Things around our neck. We shared our many similar experiences, this time with non-judgment and even less cynicism. For those two days, it felt like the grip of that "thing" was not as tight.

Could this moment be the elusive and long-awaited opportunity to do what is right? To finally exhale? Time would tell.

Raphael T. Tshibangu, M.D.

Loyalty!

It was also around this time, in 2019, that I started replaying in my mind many recent troubling events in this country. These were long existing, conveniently swept under the rug, but recently reawakened and amplified by the current president. These were issues of race, xenophobia, injustice, and inequality. Frequent news events, including the white supremacists' march in Charlottesville and Trump's supportive response, the push to limit immigration of nonwhites, the separation of families and caging of children at the Mexican border, and many more began to resuscitate in me latent, internal conflicts about belonging.

I became more introspective, once again. I started to reflect on my own personal experiences.

I was thinking about the time that a demented, bigoted patient spat in my face because he did not want his blood drawn by a black doctor, and I was glad I reacted by slapping him.

I was thinking about the time that a white police officer gave me a "speeding" ticket for dubious reasons, and I was glad I decided to fight in court and won. Was I a victim of profiling? Did he stop me because I was a black man driving an expensive Lexus? He told the judge that the reason he was interrogating me and asking me where I was from and where I was born was because I talked "funny." But I wondered, even then, if he simply assumed I was a criminal and just needed to establish or fabricate a crime.

I was thinking about the many times some white patients, who were initially assigned to me in our practice, would choose another physician stating that they preferred a woman doctor when they clearly were uncomfortable with a male black physician.

I was thinking about the time when a long-time patient who had told her daughter, whom I delivered, that she loved me, forbade the same daughter from going out with one of my "nephews" because he was a "Nigger." I wondered how she perceived me then! A tolerable Nigger? An honorary "White," as long as I stayed on my good behavior?

I was inescapably thinking about how, with the advent of Trumpism, we were witnessing the awakening and open acceptance of anti-immigrant, racist, xenophobic, and nativist sentiments, pronouncement, and actions. It was all in plain sight—with no apology! I am reminded of an unapologetic Trumpist I was scheduled to play golf with in a random-assignment golf league. "Hi, I voted for Trump and I am not politically correct" was the way he proudly introduced himself to me.

Slightly puzzled, I simply replied, "Well, the only thing we will talk about is golf." I went on and beat him that round, but I wondered if I should have had a better response to that crazy and arrogant introduction.

More and more, I began to reflect about America's actions in the world, in general, and in the DRC in particular. So much mischief, so many sins over the past 400 years. I was thinking about the CIA-assisted assassination of Patrice Lumumba, the first prime minister of the Congo, a fearless patriot, a courageous and visionary giant, a true hero. I could only painfully imagine how different the history of the Congo would have been. I was thinking about the support given to the anti-communist dictator Mobutu, for decades, as long as he was providing cover and maintaining a firewall as America's proxy in its Cold War. We are all fully aware of the damage that despot's reign caused for thirty-two years. I was thinking about the support provided to Paul Kagame of Rwanda and Yoweri Museveni of Uganda in their self-interested destabilization of the eastern part of the Congo, thus facilitating the continued pillage of Congolese resources.

I was thinking about the meddling, destabilization, and destruction in recent years of many countries, including Panama, East Timor, Iraq, Libya, and Venezuela. I was particularly shocked by the vivid chronicles of these sinful adventures in John Perkins's *Confessions of an Economic Hitman*.

I was thinking.

And the more I thought, the more I would empathize, if not identify in some way, with the victims of anti-immigration, injustice, malfeasance, oppression, and exploitation. It was yet another instance of That Thing around my neck.

I kept thinking and getting more and more disturbed—disillusioned—that what I may have seen as mere blemishes or minor imperfections on America's paradise-like façade were actually major flaws, immense shortcomings. They were like a gigantic, ugly wart that could be cauterized, at best, or an invasive and potentially metastatic cancer, at worst.

I began, again, to loathe America's myopic view of the world. I was despising the attitude and meaning of "America First," which stands for "Mine first, yours may be later." I was despising the view that there must be winners and losers; the view that, therefore, in order for us to win, somebody must lose. Like Maya Angelou, I was despising the idea of "getting mine at any cost even if it means stepping on somebody's neck."

How could I ignore this ugly side of America? Could I acknowledge it and still be a loyal citizen?

Tribalism

Like many others, I once thought that tribalism with its negative connotations was limited to so-called primitive—mostly African—and other "developing" countries like the DRC. Indeed, there are multiple examples of the destructive, murderous force of tribalism all over the world. The Balkan Wars, the perennial dispute over Kashmir, the war in Biafra, the Rwandan Genocide, and the ethnic cleansing of the Baluba from Shaba are only a few examples of tribalism's evil side.

Still fresh in my mind are the tragic, murderous events endured by the Baluba in 1991–1993, which resulted in the expulsion of over 500,000 Kasai natives from the Katanga province, over 150 dead and many more family lives disrupted. Being a Muluba, I feel that these crimes against humanity have carved an indelible scar in my psyche. Even though I was safe and secure, ten thousand miles away, many of my family members, my brothers in particular, were in the midst of this insanity and would be forever marked.

The scene was set and the seed sewn back in colonial times. Katanga was a flourishing region, with the mining companies and other modern industries built by the Belgian colonizers. Needing a sufficient and able workforce, they brought in ambitious and enterprising young people from surrounding areas, though primarily from Kasai. Over time, the Kasaiens took advantage of available resources, especially in the realm of education. This resulted in many Kasaiens reaching positions of responsibility earlier than Katanga natives. In most professions, medicine, law, engineering, aviation, and even sports, Kasaiens were always among the firsts. As it is in many other places in the world, this apparent privileged position occupied by "these foreigners" would become a source of envy, anger, and tension.

It was only a matter of time before unscrupulous, self-interested politicians would seize this opportunity to further their own agenda. Such was the case with Gabriel Kyungu wa Kumwanza, then governor of Katanga, who became a master at inciting hate and division. He started out by blaming the Kasaiens for stealing all the good jobs; he blamed them for all the socioeconomic ills experienced by the Katangese; he branded the Kasiens as parasites and cockroaches and loved to call them *bilulu* (insects) in his speeches. Like a devious demagogue, he exhorted his followers to rise up and protect their interests. "Rise up, Katanga," he said incessantly. "Katanga is for Katangese. We must fight for regional purity," became a refrain during most of 1991. Kyungu had become a cult figure and perceived savior who would be followed into hell if he so wished.

Finally, in mid-August 1992, he unleashed his gang of thugs masquerading as a political party to indiscriminately target any Kasaien with violence. The youth section of the UFERI (Union of Federalists and Independent Republicans) became a vigilante force. They were armed with machetes, spears, and Molotov cocktails and constantly incited to go kill, maim, and forcibly remove the *bilulus* from their houses, which they could then occupy.

Entire families carried what they could on their backs and sought refuge at train stations or in a few schools that offered some protection. Many families were forced into trains, which would eventually take them to poorly set-up refugee camps in Kasai. Many of the hunted, who escaped machete blows and sudden death in cities like Likasi and Kolwezi, died later, either in transit or in the refugee camps because of malnutrition, poor sanitation, and no healthcare.

Touched by these horrific events that we powerlessly witnessed from afar, a group of Congolese in the U.S. founded *Leja Bulela* (Show That You Care) in 1993 of which I became a member. It is a nonprofit organization initially set up as a reaction to these atrocities, to ensure that we did not forget, and it continues today to provide humanitarian relief to people in the Kasai province.

In light of this experience and countless others, it is sad to note that America has not been, and is not, spared from the scourge of tribalism. Maybe not as much in its original sense or ethnic base, but certainly in the manifestation of blind allegiance to a group or groupthink. We have witnessed and are witnessing it in its nefarious form right here, right now, in groups such as the Ku Klux Klan, neo-Nazis, White Supremacists, and Forever Trumpers.

Unfortunately, it is not limited to only those more vocal and belligerent groups, often considered on the fringe. On the contrary, larger and larger swaths of the population have knowingly or unknowingly become tribalistic. This has become even more obvious over the past few years as Trump's ramped-up racist, xenophobic, anti-immigrant rhetoric gave his 70-million-plus base a home. It became more visible as people took sides during Trump's impeachment proceedings; it became even more obvious during the coronavirus pandemic, as people became pro- or anti-masks; it was certainly obvious with the rise and expansion of the Black Lives Matter movement, spurred by injustice, inequality, and the shocking and blatant murders of black men and women at the hands of the police.

In the era of Trumpism in particular, we have seen a conglomeration of deplorable, miserable, unhappy individuals for whom the tribe—be it Whiteness, America First-ness, Pro-Life-ness, etc.—constitutes their world. The tribe has become their base of solidarity, social and cultural security. And even when they do not want to openly claim what is irrational and deplorable—such as electric fence walls, border cages for detainees seeking asylum, separation of children from their parents—these red-MAGA-hat-wearing Trumpists often hide behind patriotic slogans and regurgitate talking points in their speeches and pronouncements. They would rather talk about a thriving economy that, in all likelihood, is excluding others and only benefiting a few. They would rather talk about "law and order" when faced with protests and riots than address the root cause of these grievances. They would rather talk about the need for blacks to be more responsible and take care of their communities than confront the entrenched systemic and institutional racism that has led to the wide economic disparities. They would rather talk about rampant illegal immigration than face their xenophobic, racist instincts and biases.

And these tribal instincts recurrently surface every time there is a national crisis that appears to threaten their immediate material and selfish interests. Under such circumstances, they have defended—and are now more emboldened to defend—these interests with total disregard for others. With Trump as their cheerleader or their savior, they are now willing to disregard this country's rules and the institutions that support them.

I am speaking about pathetic individuals such as Representative Nunes, Senator McConnell, Senator Graham, and the like, who shamelessly demonstrated, consciously and often subconsciously, this type of blind allegiance to the tribe. Almost impermeable to reason, their psyche revolves around the dictates of the tribe even when they do not believe them. They are pitiful hypocrites, coward chameleons who have built a psychological fortress of solidarity when it comes to their perceived interests.

It may be because they do not seem to see any future, or even any survival, outside the tribe. As my brother-in-law Herman often says, "Understand that they don't have anywhere else to go." Well, whatever their individual reasons, they do not realize that this limits them intellectually and morally. They have become imbeciles, zombies, intellectually dishonest, and outright liars—or worse.

These so-called leaders have abdicated their duty to lead. Like all loyal tribesmen, they have rather blindly, sheepishly, chosen to answer to whichever demagogue holds power. Out of loyalty, or sometimes blinded by their political ambitions, they shamelessly flatter like Mike Pence; they applaud incessantly and always try to please. It is easier than doing the hard work of leading.

These behaviors were in full display during the Mueller investigation of the 2016 election meddling by Russia. We witnessed them even more so during the impeachment proceeding of Trump, at the end of which Trump was acquitted despite overwhelming evidence of wrongdoing. We witnessed impeachment witnesses such as Alexander Vindman, Fiona Hill, and other real patriots being accused of being disloyal, at best, and traitors, at worst. "They should know what we do to them, what we do to traitors," uttered some of the Trumpists.

These witnesses were being threatened with unthinkable punishments, including death. But many others were simply called disloyal and greeted with chants of "go back where you came from." Such was the case with The Squad. Representatives Ilhan Omar, Ayanna Pressley, Rashida Tlaib, and Alexandria Ocasio-Cortez are a group of freshmen, progressive congresswomen who have been speaking out against injustice, inequality, and racial economic and health disparities; calling for justice and police reform; and demanding better stewardship of the environment. How could anyone be against such goals? Why and how would anyone accuse them of being disloyal, unpatriotic, and worth of banishment to whatever "shitholes" they came from?

How could the Trumpists be so blind? How could there be so many?

Navigating these confusing times was stressful, to say the least. I recall one such moment during the summer. I was driving to a golf course about fifteen miles from home. Almost at my destination, I realized that I had forgotten my wallet, which contained my driver's license. I suddenly became anxious as I tried to figure out what I would say or do if I got stopped by the police. Should I go back? Should I ask Sherry to bring me my wallet or at least be on standby? I became more anxious when I realized that she was also playing golf at a different course and was not reachable for several hours. I decided to go on and made sure I stayed in my lane and under the speed limit. It was striking to note that previously, on many occasions, when I would rush to work and forget my wallet at home, I never experienced such dread. I guessed it was a sign of the time.

As my level of unease, distress, confusion, and disgust for these racists, bigots, and selfish xenophobes was hitting a crescendo, I inevitably started questioning my own Americanness. How do the nativists see me? How do I fit in? More than fifty years in America, thirty-six as a law-abiding, tax-paying, civic-minded citizen, would they ask me to go back where he came from if I spoke up? Would they tell me to go back to my "DRC shithole" if I disagreed with them?

I was questioning my loyalty to America in light of the strong negative feelings I was now harboring about America's past and current sins, as well as my strong disagreement with many of the current administration's policies. Is my loyalty conditional? And how strong is that loyalty when at the same time I feel loyal to the Congo and have similar, strong feelings of attachment despite its gigantic problems? I can hear in my head accusations of dual loyalty at best and disloyalty at worst. And although I do not feel afraid of arrest or persecution, I know it would be disturbing and hurtful to be perceived as ungrateful or treasonous. Why is it that one has to renounce one's cherished community in favor of another simply to demonstrate loyalty to one or the other? Surely I can be loyal to the soul of America and work to "Build Back Better" like President Biden would say, and at the same time heed the call of President Tshisekedi to resuscitate the Congo and "Build it Together"?

Realizations

The recent presidential elections, the Black Lives Matter movement, and the coronavirus pandemic have given many of us an opportunity for reflection and introspection. Like many others, I too have had my realizations.

I firmly realized that, rather than being monolithic, America is not only diverse but deeply polarized. There are extremely strong feelings on each side of the divide and often very little room for compromise. Little room, because there is often little understanding and little empathy for each other's positions; little room, because the prevailing attitude remains one of win-lose rather than win-win. Each tribe feels like doing whatever it takes to protect their interests, and in order for them to win the other side must lose or be demonized.

I realized that tribesmen subscribe to groupthink and that most do not think at all but sheepishly follow and blindly do what they are asked to do.

It behooves us to be more and better informed. Given our diversity, it behooves us to truly listen more to and hear one other; it behooves us to understand that compromise is not a sign of weakness or synonymous with failure, but rather a way to advance interests that may not be perfectly aligned.

As such, I do not believe in uninformed loyalty; I do not believe in blind loyalty; I do not believe in unconditional loyalty. Just like Samantha Power, Fiona Hill, and many other first-generation immigrants—who had recently been accused of being disloyal because they dared raise their voice to speak out against injustice, unjust wars, presidential malfeasance—theirs and mine is mindful, enlightened, and patriotic loyalty. Theirs and mine is deliberate, thoughtful, and chosen loyalty. It is loyalty to the ideal of America, the best of America, and not to an individual, a particular president, a particular administration, or a particular tribe.

It is loyalty to what America *should* and could be, rather than blind loyalty that is tribalistic and divisive. It is more loyalty than witnessed in so many of the native-born Americans who are totally ignorant of what specific values bind them together; it is more loyalty because it deliberately supports the values of what is, for most of us (except for the few Native Americans), the New Homeland; it is more loyalty because it voluntarily chooses to protect those values and speaks out when they are threatened; it is more loyalty because it requires us to stay vigilant and to keep our eyes open.

It does not dictate blind allegiance, but rather demands courageous voices and actions when the Homeland is straying from its path.

Hopefully, when these questions arise in the future, I will keep reminding myself that America was an idea born of principles, not based upon historical relationships or tribal politics. America's ideal includes the promotion of rights and values including "life, liberty, and the pursuit of happiness" as well as freedom of speech, religion, and enterprise. To that America I say, "Yes!" To that America I am loyal and will remain so, as long as it continues to be a beacon of hope for the world, a magnet for the world's best and brightest, and as needed a refuge for the oppressed and disenfranchised. To tribal politics, world policing or bullying, oppressive and exploited native imperialism, I say, "No!"

I will also remind myself that right now America is undergoing its version of a burning house. As someone said, "When your house is burning, you would do what it takes to extinguish the fire, even if it means pouring water on the furniture, carpet, or any other household items. However, any reasonable person who did not witness the fire or the smoke would later look at the damp furniture and conclude that you do not love your house or do not take care of your house. They would look at the majestic house still standing yet don't appreciate the efforts you made to save it." Well, America, our majestic house is on fire. So let us be mindful, enlightened loyal citizens. Let us resist our tribal instincts when they rear their heads. As much as possible, let us remind ourselves that in the end, we are all equal regardless of culture, religion, occupation, or class, with inalienable human rights. We are all connected despite our borders, and something that affects one person has an effect on another. We should resist the temptation to win at the expense of another but rather be of benefit to one another. We should think of win-win and resist the temptation to feel tall by keeping others on their knees. Let us let America be almighty, all powerful, but at the same time be a force for good; let Her be so, not by oppressing, stealing, or stepping on other people's necks, but with dignity and respect.

Finally, I will remind myself that I am Congolese and the Congo is and will remain an undeniable part of me. I love the DRC and will continue to look for ways I can assist in its rebuilding.

But I am also an American and I love America. I will criticize and disagree with policies when I must, despite the increasingly loud chants of "go back where you came from." I am here to stay. I am not going anywhere. This is Home.

So to my fellow immigrants, my extended family:

To those who have struggled to belong and struggled to get That Thing off our neck, understand that we cannot sacrifice so much—some risking limb and life—and just be content that we have arrived. We have to take advantage of all the opportunities this land provides.

We also cannot just be content that we have achieved our own American Dream.

Part of the dream should be to keep the Statue of Liberty shining and welcoming; to keep America beautiful; to keep America standing as a force for good; to keep America from becoming the modern-day colonizer.

We have to be grateful to America, but must keep Her from becoming the world bully who deceives, disinforms in order to exploit, disrupts, and destroys when she does not get her way or simply when it pleases Her.

We can be proud of America and still be able to denounce the wrong doings.

We can do all of these things without becoming disloyal or being accused of ingratitude, at best, or treason, at worst.

We can do these things without losing our souls and without becoming the new tribal sentinels and gatekeepers who want to keep other would-be immigrants out.

We can also do all of these things without erasing, deleting, who we are, including where we came from.

Raphael T. Tshibangu, M.D.

ON GRATITUDE

From time to time I had asked myself, "Is this all there is to life?" I had even read Rabbi Harold Kushner's *When All You've Ever Wanted Isn't Enough* in an effort to find some answers and gain a better understanding of why—no matter our fortunes, no matter our station in life—there always seems to be a need to search for more. Seemingly never satisfied, we keep looking for or asking for whatever appears to be eluding us at the moment.

I know I am not alone in this respect, but this introspective journey has allowed me to partially address these questions of lack, or "never enough," or perpetual "unsatisfaction."

As I wrote this memoir, I thought about the many years of schooling; the long hours of hard work I put in for years; the sleepless nights, especially during medical school and during my residency. After almost forty years of Obstetrics and Gynecology practice, I have no doubt that I worked hard, even harder than most. How many things I deprived myself of; how many parties, celebrations, vacations were given up so that I could get my work done?

I reflected about the untold, immeasurable, emotional cost I paid along the way, being separated from my family at the age of eleven and from my country and my childhood friends at seventeen. How heavy the price of loneliness and homesickness, as I remembered almost always celebrating in silence or suffering alone in silence. I wondered, with some irritation, that while I yearned to be with my DRC family, be among them, it sometimes seemed like they were content with the arrangement, as long as I was providing. Strangely, I thought, some are most likely emotionally happier than I, despite their apparent poverty and my apparent wealth.

I acknowledged the courage, determination, endurance, and resilience that my journey required and the obstacles that I had to overcome to achieve my American Dream.

Surely, I deserve what I have; I should be content and happy.

And yet, this thought will often pop up with a thick veil of disappointment because I did not quite realize my desired outcome. I was Dr. Rieux in my dreams for twenty-plus years, preparing to tackle the "plague," but in the end I am not Rieux and the plagues—Ebola, COVID, typhoid, malaria, and many other scourges and ailments—are still with us.

More Realizations

In late September 2019, a close friend, Renée Thomas, had invited us to a christening event in London, England, for her first grandchild. Her daughter Annina had been living there for many years and had given birth a couple of months earlier. We were eager to see all of them, so we accepted the invitation. We thought it would be even more exhilarating if we could pay a surprise visit to our daughter and family in Austria. With excitement, we hastily planned the trip, and, before long, we were landing at Vienna airport. It was very early morning on October 6, my birthday.

We rented a vehicle for the one-and-a-half-hour drive to Fürstenfeld, where they reside. Upon arrival, we parked the car on the street in front of the house. We walked to the back of the house where a large, double-glass sliding door, facing a covered porch, lead to the kitchen and dining room inside. As we started approaching the doors, Titi was making her entrance into the kitchen area. She was coming in from the foyer. She suddenly froze, as she gazed through the glass door and saw us. Fearing a ghostly apparition, she quickly retreated, not believing her eyes. A few seconds later, she came back, gingerly. She took a peak and then another. She slowly advanced. "Dad? Ma?" she said incredulously.

"Yes," we responded with a smile. Finally trusting her eyes and her ears, she opened the door and we hugged warmly and tenderly.

Soon after, Elena came running down from her upstairs bedroom. Startled by our presence, she instinctively jumped into her mother's arms rather than ours, as she had done many times before. She glanced at us and looked at her mother for reassurance.

"Kambo Granny?" We all acquiesced. Miraculously, her startled, puzzled look changed into the beautiful angelic smile we often crave and look forward to. Danny and Thomas, my son-in-law, came next—still surprised but not as shocked. Overall, the moment was priceless. It was a wonderful surprise. It was worth the trip.

We had no other agenda for our visit. We simply engaged in mundane activities, such as shopping, cooking, and taking the kids to and from school. Who would believe that such ordinary daily chores could be so enjoyable?

On our third day, we decided to spend most of our time at a local, luxurious thermal spa resort (Therme Loipersdorf, Austria) that offered multiple water activities and spa services. The water at the Therme is naturally warm, soft, rich in minerals and has a silky, slippery feel. As Danny, Elena, and I moved from activity to activity, from water tube slides to floating inflated canoes, I noticed that the floors and the stairs were slippery and treacherous. I kept admonishing the ever-energetic Danny, who was always eager to get to the next ride and could not resist the urge to run.

An hour or so later, comfortable in my surroundings, I neglected to hold on to the rails as recommended. As I came down the slippery concrete stairs in search of Danny, it happened. In a fraction of a millisecond, I slipped. I briefly heard a loud thump, as I slid down to the bottom of the stairs. Everything was dark for a second except for flickering yellowish, bright lights. I was suddenly lying on the floor in the fetal position. One of the kids started talking to me. "Are you okay? Are you okay?" He quickly left and just as quickly returned with one of the resort's attendants. Kneeling next to me, the attendant asked again and again if I was okay.

"Should we get the ambulance?" he asked. I was slow to respond, somewhat reluctant to do anything at that moment. He must have been worried about my head, as he asked with grave concern, "How is your head?"

Indeed, I had barely avoided banging my head on the concrete and only managed to graze its menacing edges on my way down. But my head seemed fine, so I replied, "It is not my head, it is my back." I must have slipped and fallen on my buttock, sending a jolt through my spine while portions of my mid back were getting battered against the edges of the stairs.

"Can you move?" he asked.

"No, not yet," I replied. I was only temporarily paralyzed by the pain and spasms in my back and certainly did not feel like moving. He asked if I could move my toes, and I was glad to realize that I could. I could move not just my toes but could feel and gently move both of my lower extremities.

Several minutes later, I was lying down on a treatment table in the spa's infirmary. With ice on my back and ibuprofen on board, I was finally able to crack a smile at Sherry and the kids who were anxiously standing around me. I remember saying, "Boy, I was lucky!"

I know now that I meant to say I was "grateful." Minutes prior, I was millimeters away from a concussion, maybe a broken skull, a broken back, or worse. Instead, all I seemed to have was a sore back, a slow gait, and a headache. And sure enough, X-rays taken much later because of persistent back pain and spasms, showed there were no fractures. They confirmed that I had sustained only bruising, contusions, and spasms that could be reasonably relieved by anti-inflammatories and tramadol.

Thankfully, the remainder of our stay in Austria was uneventful and wonderful. I was and I remain grateful.

A few days later, we were in London where we spent some time sightseeing, but most importantly attended the christening celebration for Georgia, Renée's granddaughter. It was a scrumptious, all-day affair. We feasted all afternoon on multiple delicacies, a fusion of Mediterranean and Middle Eastern cuisines. We ended the evening with dessert, drinking, and dancing. It was thoroughly enjoyable communing with everybody. We were delighted to have participated.

Our return flight was scheduled to go from London to Zurich, Switzerland, and on to Toronto, Canada. After a smooth check-in at Heathrow, we were tucked in comfortably in our sparsely populated business-class seats. We were close to the front of the plane. Sherry was sitting across the aisle from me, as there were many empty seats. We took off smoothly and gently cut through the slightly thick morning air without a glitch.

As soon as we reached the cruising altitude and began settling in our seats, we heard an extremely loud noise, a sharp and explosive sound. It was quickly followed by a sudden jerking of the plane, which then started to sway from side to side as it quickly lost altitude. This was no weather event! This was not the occasional turbulence we have experienced many times before! Sherry and I looked at each other as she unbuckled her seat belt and came to sit next to me. We held hands and did not say much. Sherry prayed, as she would tell me later. Shortly after the bang, one of the flight crew members came into the cabin and peaked out the window on the left side of the plane. We were about to ask her what was happening, but she quickly returned to her post. A few minutes later, which seemed like an eternity, the plane seemed stable but continued to lose altitude. Then, in a brief announcement, the captain informed us that we had lost the left engine; we needed to land urgently. He added that we were not going to make it to Zurich, but thankfully Paris Charles de Gaulle Airport was nearby.

We remained mostly quiet but anxious, unaware of what had transpired to cause the engine failure. We could feel the plane descending. As we approached the airport, the captain told us that we would land in a remote area of the tarmac. "No reason to be concerned. It is simply a precaution." Of course, we were concerned. But, strangely enough, both Sherry and I maintained a calm and seemingly fearless demeanor. We must have realized that we were powerless.

As we touched down, the plane was closely followed and then surrounded by a dozen vehicles, most of them being fire trucks, as well as law enforcement. Still puzzled but immensely relieved, we evacuated quickly but orderly.

We would later learn that the left engine had burned out for yet unknown reasons and the crew was concerned about the possibility of fire engulfing the plane. "This has never happened before," said one of our flight attendants, as she handed out business cards and pamphlets for "those who may have experienced psychological trauma and need counseling." Only then did I truly realize how close we were to a disastrous ending. We had dodged another bullet, it seemed.

It was not until all arrangements were made for our flight to Toronto that we were finally able to crack a smile. I said, "Boy, we are lucky. We avoided a fire and we landed safely!" Was it luck or God's Grace? I believe it was the latter, and for that, I am grateful.

Both of these incidents, only a few days apart, made me realize again how fragile life is. Both instances reminded me again that the course of life can change in an instant, sometimes leading to a perilous ending, sometimes not. Why and how we are spared from such an outcome is a mystery, but a stark reminder that we are promised nothing and should be grateful for everything. Grateful, not just for life, not just for the big things, but for everything—all the small things and acts of kindness that we often take for granted or think we are entitled to.

This lesson on gratitude was further expanded shortly following this otherwise fantastic trip. It was during my most recent trip to the DRC in November 2019. As noted earlier, I visited and reunited with dozens of relatives and friends. Wherever I stopped—Kinshasa, Lubumbashi, Likasi, Mbuji-Mayi—circumstances were the same. Same conversations about hardship and misery. Different faces, but similar stories and same expectations. Having learned from previous trips, I brought with me several thousand dollars in cash, which I planned to give and *wanted* to give. It was expected, it was needed, and just as importantly, it would bring me joy.

While in Mbuji-Mayi, about a dozen of my relatives—including my two sisters, their spouses, children, and grandchildren—gathered at a friend's building where I was staying. We talked, laughed, and reminisced over a long brunch that included eggs, ham, bread, tea, soft drinks, and beer. By any measure, this was quite a treat for most of them. It was an enjoyable moment for me. At the conclusion of the gathering, never sure of the best way to handle the money situation, how and how much to give to each individual, I decided to give to those present $300 each, except for my two sisters, who received a separate envelope with a more generous amount. As I finished handing out about a total of $10,000, a nephew's wife, whom I had just met, brandished the $300 with one hand while the other hand rested on her protuberant, pregnant belly. "What can I do with this? I am expecting my baby any day now. This will not even cover the hospital bill. How come I am getting the same amount as everyone else?" And she went on and on.

Understanding of her predicament, I reached again in my handbag and brought out $200 more, which I gave her. "Come on, Uncle, this is all I get?" She went on pleading and this time, gesticulating as well. "I am having a baby. This is not enough. What am I going to do with this?" she said as she held the $500 up in my face, seemingly disgusted. Feelings of disappointment, anger, and disbelief came over me. I was suddenly no longer sympathetic.

I grabbed the $500 she still held in her outstretched hand. "Well, since you do not know what to do with this, this is what *I* can do with it," I tersely said. I took the money and divided it among five of the youngest children who were still in attendance. I said to the kids, "Hopefully, you know what to do with this."

They said, "Thank you," with a smile.

I smiled back. As my newly acquired niece was pleading, "But, Uncle, what about me? What about me?" I had started to adjourn the meeting and the rest of the family and I were already saying our goodbyes. We went our separate ways.

A short time later, and intermittently during the rest of my trip, I reflected on this exchange. I could not believe the display of insolence and ingratitude. Even though I had heard similar stories from others and had similar experiences in the past, none were so brazen, none were to this degree, and none affected me as much as this one. I was willingly and joyfully giving some of my hard-earned money. I had no expectation in return. Maybe a smile? Maybe even a simple thank-you from the recipient? I knew that whatever I gave will not be enough. I had heard a thousand reasons why it is never enough. Their needs are so enormous that I had no illusions that whatever I gave would be sufficient to satisfy them. But in this country, where the average individual monthly income is $80, I thought that my gift was a rather significant and not to be looked at with such a public display of disdain.

I reflected on my response and wondered whether my niece overplayed her hand. I wondered if this was simply an exaggeration of an erroneous but commonly held belief in the Congo—and many African countries—that "There is more where that came from." and "If you do not ask you will not receive." So, she asked. And when I responded positively, she was emboldened, and continued to ask instead of being satisfied with what she had already received.

I concluded that, although partially motivated by anger, my reaction was quite appropriate. I thought it was a good lesson for this young relative. And I must admit that I was somewhat tickled when I replayed the scene in my head and watched her face turn pale when she realized that she was truly going to end up with nothing.

More significantly, this interaction made me think about myself and about those times when I would look at my life and ask disappointingly, "Is this all there is?" I now understand what an expression of ingratitude that question is in my situation. How could I be so lacking in appreciation and recognition for what God, the Source, the Universe has given me? How could I not appreciate all the blessings that had been bestowed upon me?

I recalled a meeting with one of my childhood friends in Likasi. He was our neighbor in Trabeka, and our families were very close. Despite our very close relationship and friendship in primary school,

I could not have recognized him in a million years except for the context of our meeting and a few recollections of our childhood adventures. He was walking with a limp, painfully. He was emaciated and edentulous. With torn shoes on his feet, he was wearing a white shirt that appeared almost rusty due to prolonged exposure to the ever-present dust that could not be washed away. However, he was genuinely ecstatic to see me. I, on the other hand, was glad to see him but also somewhat sad inside, contrary to my outward expressions. Sad to see the predicament he was in, sad to think that this could have been me. I recall thinking then, "I hope he has a happy life." But our time together was brief. We did not spend enough time for me to find out whether or not he was happy. I wondered about him and his outward appearance. I wondered about many more like him. How many are truly happy? How many would have been happier somewhere else, under better conditions. How many would have taken another path but did not have a choice, did not have the opportunity? I, on the other hand, had the opportunity to leave this small, suffocating, crumbling little town. I, on the other hand, had the good fortune to not only escape but to prosper.

I had benefited from the generosity of my father's friends who sheltered me and helped me during my last years in primary school. I benefited from the generosity of my older brother Alphonse who provided me with a safe place, a refuge, during my time away from boarding school. I was a beneficiary of the generosity of strangers many times, including those who contributed to my scholarship for Karavia, my scholarship to Amherst College, and my scholarship to the University of Rochester. I benefited from the generosity of Dr. Van Huysen who spared me the anxiety of going through the matching system for my residency program. I had an unsolicited opportunity to work with the Rochester Medical Group when it became clear that going back to the Congo was not a viable option.

Of course, as I have pointed out, I know I worked hard and sacrificed much along the way. No doubt, I paid a price. However, were it not for the opportunities afforded me, often from unknown sources, none of my accomplishments would have been possible. What would I have become? It is impossible to tell and also unnecessary to ask. There are, and will be, no do-overs.

What is clear now is that I owe a great deal of gratitude to so many and for so much. I am grateful for life, cut short for so many of my childhood friends, Cele, Morceau, Tshiany, Yayop. I am grateful for every day, realizing that the future is not guaranteed, and that each day is a gift. I am grateful for my health, despite many aches and pains—achy backs, knees, shoulders—I am thankful I am still able to do many things I enjoy, such as golf and yoga. I am grateful for my abundance despite the understandable natural desire for more. I am grateful for my family—for all the moments of joy they have given me, the support they have given me, and the meaning and purpose they have given to my life. I am grateful for all the blessings and many more.

To the question, "Is this all there is?" I can now sincerely, humbly, and gratefully say that despite its sham, drudgery, and broken dreams, it is still a wonderful world. And, as I try to be cheerful and continue to strive to be happy, I will remember to say, "Thank you, and thank you for everything!"

With few regrets, but full of appreciation…

Raphael T. Tshibangu, M.D.

Epilogue

When in late 2019, I set out to chronicle my Congo–American journey, I could not imagine the earth-shattering events that were about to unfold and how impactful they would be for anybody with eyes to see and/or ears to listen.

As I pointed out a few pages earlier, these episodes have affected me and affected many others differently, in ways we may and may not be aware of.

I am obviously talking about the unrelenting and devastating coronavirus pandemic, the crescendo of the Black Lives Matter (BLM) movement, the culmination of Trumpism which led to a failed insurrection and a second impeachment of D.J. Trump.

It is not my objective to recount these historical events, but a brief summary may provide more context to the points made and lessons learned.

First identified in Wuhan, China, the novel coronavirus quickly became a global pandemic. From its emergence in the United States, it became clear that although the virus spared no one, it disproportionately affected—and still does—the elderly and those with preexisting conditions such as diabetes, asthma, cardiovascular diseases, and obesity. More strikingly but not surprisingly the devastating effects of the virus were more prominent in the African-American, Hispanic, and Native American communities where the mortality rate is three to four times higher. This tragic reality can be partially explained by preexisting and still persistent healthcare disparities; limited testing in poor neighborhoods leading to unsuspected chain transmission in overpopulated housing; low-budget, low-quality, and under-resourced minority-serving institutions; tenuous economic conditions forcing many of the minorities to constitute the bulk of the essential—sacrificial—workers including transportation, retail, meat plant, and home healthcare workers who are obliged to work as long as they can stand on their feet.

These issues of limited access to care and discriminatory treatment when care is available are certainly part of the long existent and widespread institutional racism as well as injustice that the BLM movement has been trying to address.

Founded in 2013, the BLM movement was brought about to protest against the incidents of police brutality and racially motivated violence against black people including Trayvon Martin, Michael Brown, Eric Garner, and others who died in police custody. With the public murder of George Floyd in the summer of 2020, what may have been only a slogan for some became a global movement, as international attention was drawn to the plight of the black man with a white person's knee on his neck. Calls for racial equality and criminal justice reform were disingenuously minimized because of the protests, and it remains to be seen if they were heard.

I said disingenuously, but hypocritically may be more appropriate, considering the reaction of law enforcement to the Trump-incited insurrectionists who invaded the capitol on January 6, 2021. Any honest observer would easily conclude that if these were supporters of the BLM movement, the Capitol hallways would have turned into rivers of blood.

That was a naked example of racism and unequal treatment for the whole world to see.

And as incredible as this incident may have been, it was not entirely surprising considering the toxic rhetoric that characterized Trump's administration and his ill-fated election.

The confluence of these phenomena led me to the realizations that I expanded on in the previous pages and only reinforced them. By exposing the true face of America, its potential grandeur—but also its flaws, weaknesses, and imperfections—it reinforced the need to maintain a high awareness about these socioeconomic disparities, inequalities, and injustices. We need to remain vigilant so that we can speak up when we can and, more importantly, act when we must.

Coincidentally, the pandemic that was ravaging the world, and the U.S. in particular, was also striking the DRC, but thankfully not as hard. Can you imagine the carnage it could have unleashed in a country of 80 million with less than 1,000 ventilators?

In any case, early in the pandemic, an extraordinary moment in the DRC history, watched throughout the country and across the globe, was unfolding. It was the trial of the century, the trial of Vital Kamerhe. Then-President Tshisekedi's Chief of Staff, Kamerhe was a veteran politician, a power broker, a king maker. With a thirty-year political career, including a recent presidential bid, he was considered untouchable. When he was accused of embezzling about $50 million that was earmarked for social housing projects, part of Tshisekedi's 100-day program, there was immense disappointment about persistent corruption but not much surprise. With a shrug of the shoulders, people felt it was more of the same, despite recent campaign promises, and nothing would come of it. After all, he was the most senior politician ever targeted for corruption and a close associate of the President. So, when he was arrested on April 8, 2020 and kept in jail without bail, shock waves reverberated throughout the nation as people witnessing the first high profile political figures to face charges of embezzlement and corruption.

Because of COVID-19 restrictions, this unprecedented landmark trial was held in open air and broadcasted on RTNC (*Radio-Télévision nationale congolaise*). The uninterrupted coverage gripped the attention of a population determined to break with the past and impatient for change in governance. Being mostly confined to the house during this time, I was one of those who closely followed these outdoor court proceedings with eager anticipation.

Kamerhe remained defiant, even in his prison blue-and-yellow jacket. Convinced of his untouchability, he repeatedly sidelined his attorneys and addressed the judges with arrogance. As expected, he professed his innocence and predicted his imminent release. The judges and state attorneys who were enduring the warm temperatures under their voluminous black robes, corona masks, and white vinyl gloves, were not impressed nor intimidated. They remained probing in their questions and were undeterred even after the mysterious murder of the Chief Judge one week into the trial.

Although the evidence against Kamerhe and his accomplices was clear and overwhelming, the final verdict was not certain, given a long history of justice miscarriage. This time however, people cheered when on June 11, this once-powerful political giant was found guilty and sentenced to twenty years in prison.

The people's desire to see the country on a path to the rule of law, its yearning to end the cancerous rampant corruption, was palpable during the trial and certainly following the verdict. Was *"L'état de droit"* (a state of law) finally here? The beginning of the end of corruption? Many people hoped so. I, too, saw another ray of hope for the DRC.

Clearly, this was not the time for me to *let go*.

My introspective journey so far had revealed to me that I can't let go of the DRC, just like I can't let go of my family. I do not want to let go and I see no reason to let go. In spite of distance and the passage of time, in spite of the influences of modernization—good and bad—despite the ravages inflicted by men and nature (disease, sickness, wars, exploitation, looting, bad governance); despite the seemingly never ending misery and pain, I can't let go. I can't let go of Hope. "Hope is the thing with feathers that perches in the soul, and sings the tune without the words, and never stops at all." (Emily Dickinson). Hope, that with perseverance, this young, resilient, creative, ingenious people will one day soon reach its fullest socioeconomic and human potential; hope that soon they will all share in and finally enjoy the scandalously abundant and enviable riches this vast country has been blessed with.

I can't let go of the vibrant culture often obscured, ignored, or lost when faced with real-life concerns about hunger, pain, and misery. I would rather celebrate the rich diversity of colorful languages: Tshiluba, Lingala, Swahili, and Kikongo; the prolific and exciting works of art as expressed in world-renowned sculptures, wood carvings, paintings, and pottery; the much imitated Congolese music that has exhilarated, romanced, and uplifted people around the world; and certainly, the food and cuisine, which is often fresh and organic, simple and complex at the same time, enriched and enhanced by flavorful spices.

I can't let go of the enchanting, thick, and warm smell of the earth that lingers in the air after a warm rain.

I can't let go because it is in my soul. It is *all* in my soul.

This journey, which has taken me from ambiguity and anguish to a zone of possibilities and enlightenment—and even happiness—has been a cathartic and healing exercise. It has reassured me that "Can't Let Go," as sung by Jonathan Butler, does not have to be a source of melancholy. The lyrics no longer suggest that I should live in the past, nostalgically anguishing about what could have been. They no longer suggest that I should take responsibility for all my country's and my family's problems, or unreasonably, foolishly, take on the burden of solving all ills. Instead, the song and the lyrics motivate me to do what I am truly able to do—what I internally and honestly feel capable of doing. Rather than relying on others' approval or criticism to dictate what and how much I do, my own values, which have guided me reasonably well so far, will remain the major determinant. "Enough" will not be what other people tell me is enough, since there is always one more cause to support, one more person to feed or heal, one more animal to rescue.

Furthermore, to paraphrase the Desiderata, in matters of giving back, just like in many areas of life, I will not compare myself to others, for there will always be greater and lesser than me, better and worse than me.

In practical terms, I intend to refocus my attention on the RTST Foundation and use it as a vehicle in our efforts to promote better education and healthcare in the DRC as well as our immediate community. I will continue to support my family, focusing more on providing them with the tools they may need for their success. Whenever possible, Sherry and I will continue to support organizations that work to remedy inequities in education and healthcare areas; organizations such as Action for a Better Community (ABC), the Urban League Black Scholars Program, the Rochester Area Community Foundation (RACF), Monroe Community College Foundation, the Highland Hospital Foundation, Doctors Without Borders, the African Leadership Academy, and many others. At the same time, I will gratefully enjoy the blessings that I have been given and worked for without much guilt or regret while I strive to do well and do good for my family, my community, my adopted country, my Homeland.

Raphael T. Tshibangu, M.D.

Appendix

Famille Tshibangu
Family Chart
List of Family Members

Bibliography

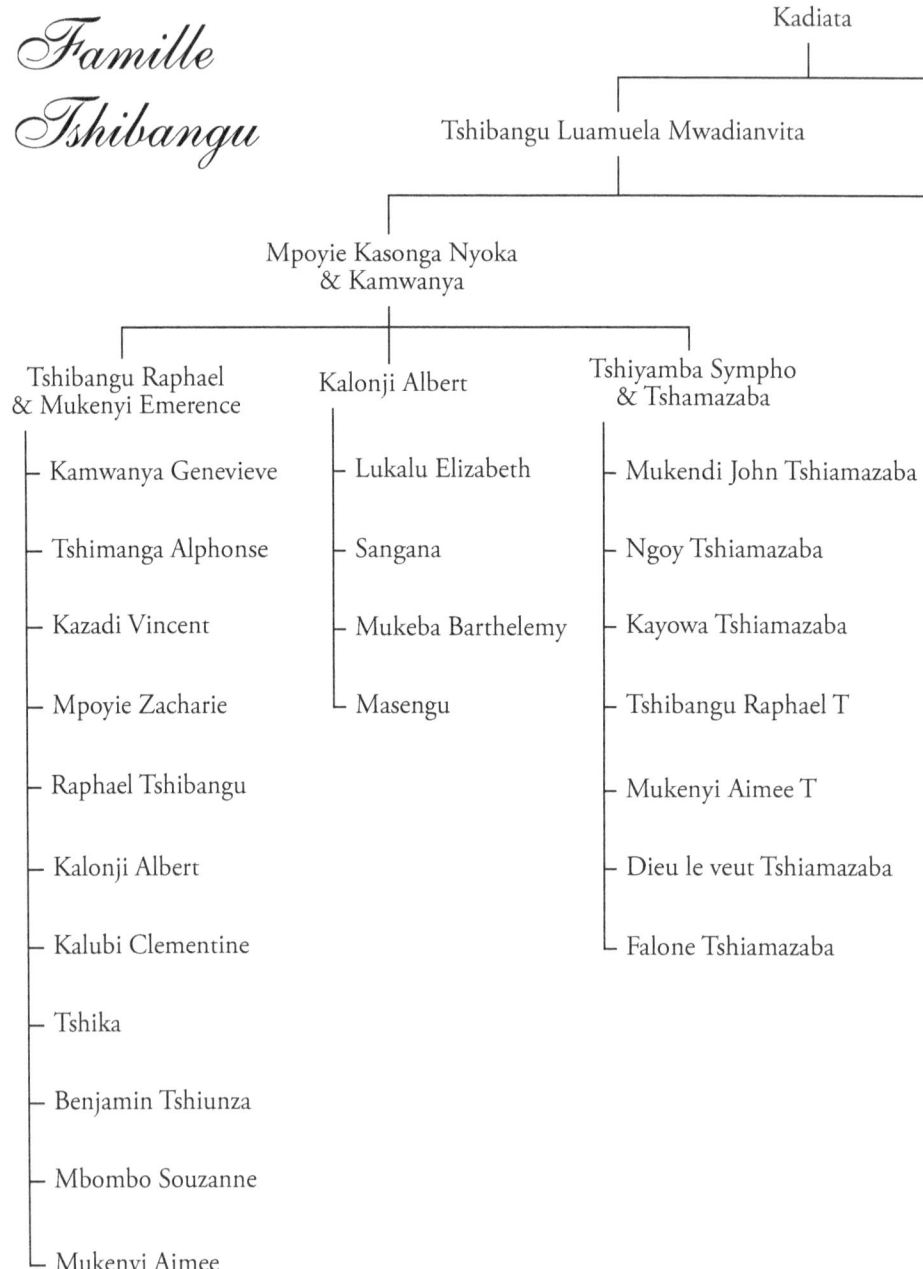

Raphael T. Tshibangu, M.D.

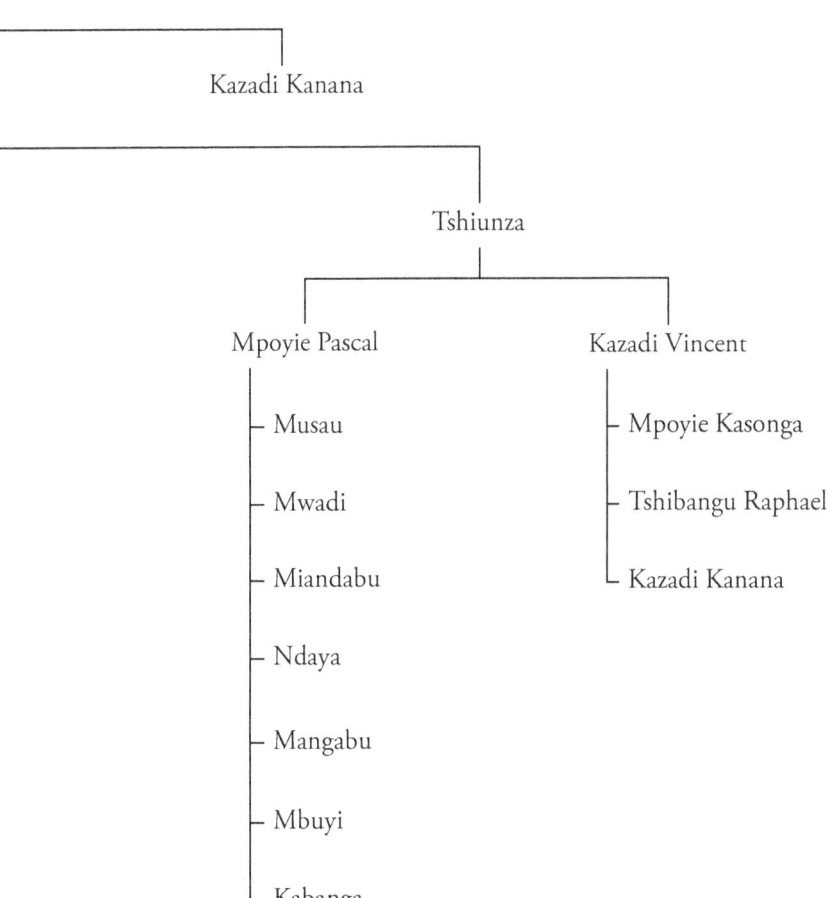

Famille Tshibangu

Great-Great-Grandfather
1 Kadiata + ??
1.1 Tshibangu Luamuela Mwadianvita
1.2 Kazadi Kanana

Great-Grandfather
1.1 Tshibangu Luamuela Mwadianvita + ??
1.1.1. Mpoyie Kasonga Nyoka
1.1.2 Tshiunza (great-uncle)

About This List of Family Members

In our culture, it is customary to honor a person by giving a child that person's full name. In recent years, a common surname or family name is sometimes added. As clearly noted in this tree, many of the names are carried on from generation to generation.

1 = Progenitor	* = USA
1.1 = Firstborn child of 1	** = Sweden
1.1.1 = Firstborn child of 1.1	*** = South Africa
1.1.2 = Second-born child of 1.1	**** = Canada
1.2 = Second-born child of 1	***** = Austria
?? = Spouse's name unknown, to be filled in with future research	

Grandfather
1.1.1 Mpoyie Kasonga Nyoka + Kamwanya
1.1.1.1 Tshibangu Raphael
1.1.1.2 Kalonji Albert
1.1.1.3 Tshiyamba Sympho

1.1.2 Tshiunza + ??
1.1.2.1 Mpoyie Pascal
1.1.2.2 Kazadi Vincent

Parents & Siblings
1.1.1.1 Tshibangu Raphael + Mukenyi Emerence
1.1.1.1.1 Kamwanya Genevieve
1.1.1.1.2 Tshimanga Alphonse
1.1.1.1.3 Kazadi Vincent
1.1.1.1.4 Mpoyie Zacharie
1.1.1.1.5 Tshibangu Raphael*
1.1.1.1.6 Kalonji Albert*
1.1.1.1.7 Kalubi Clementine
1.1.1.1.8 Tshika
1.1.1.1.9 Benjamin Tshiunza
1.1.1.1.10 Mbombo Souzanne**
1.1.1.1.11 Mukenyi Aimee

Uncles, Aunts & Cousins
1.1.1.2 Kalonji Albert + ??
1.1.1.2.1 Lukalu Elizabeth
1.1.1.2.2 Sangana

1.1.1.2.3 Mukeba Barthelemy

1.1.1.2.4 Masengu

1.1.1.3 Tshiyamba Sympho + Tshamazaba

1.1.1.3.2 Mukendi John Tshiamazaba

1.1.1.3.3 Ngoy Tshiamazaba

1.1.1.3.4 Kayowa Tshiamazaba

1.1.1.3.5 Tshibangu Raphael Tshiamazaba

1.1.1.3.6 Mukenyi Aimee Tshiamazaba

1.1.1.3.7 Dieu le veut Tshiamazaba

1.1.1.3.8 Falone Tshiamazaba

1.1.2.1 Mpoyie Pascal

1.1.2.1.1 Musau

1.1.2.1.2 Mwadi

1.1.2.1.3 Miandabu

1.1.2.1.4 Ndaya

1.1.2.1.5 Mangabu

1.1.2.1.6 Mbuyi

1.1.2.1.7 Kabanga

1.1.2.2 Kazadi Vincent

1.1.2.2.1 Mpoyie Kasonga

1.1.2.2.1 Tshibangu Raphael

1.1.2.2.1 Kazadi Kanana

Siblings & Their Children

1.1.1.1.1 Kamwanya Genevieve + Laurent Tshibangu

1.1.1.1.1.1 Tshibangu Raphael***

1.1.1.1.1.2 Mukenyi Aimee

1.1.1.1.1.3 Mukeba Baron

1.1.1.1.1.4 Ngomba

1.1.1.1.1.5 Paco

1.1.1.1.2 Tshimanga Alphonse + Ngomba

1.1.1.1.2.1 Tshimanga Tresor

1.1.1.1.2.2 Mukenyi Aimee

1.1.1.1.3 Kazadi Kanana Vincent

1.1.1.1.3.1 Mukenyi Noella Kazadi***

1.1.1.1.3.2 Mukeba Joe Kazadi****

1.1.1.1.3.3 Mpunga Cocco Kazadi*

1.1.1.1.3.4 Christine Kamwanya Kazadi

1.1.1.1.3.5 Felie Kazadi

1.1.1.1.4 Mpoyie Zacharie Kasonga

1.1.1.1.4.1 Bertin Mpoyie

1.1.1.1.4.2 Rachel Kamwanya

1.1.1.1.4.3 Raphael Tshibangu

1.1.1.1.4.4 Mukenyi

1.1.1.1.4.5 Mwewa

1.1.1.1.4.6 Kazadi

1.1.1.1.5 Tshibangu Raphael Mwadianvita Tshisambusambu + Sherry Perry
1.1.1.1.5.1 Titi Kamawanya Muller*****

1.1.1.1.6 Kalonji Albert Tshikala + Odette Kabongo*
1.1.1.1.6.1 Tshimanga Tresor/Trey "ChiChi"*
1.1.1.1.6.2 Kamwanya Chanelle "Channy"*

1.1.1.1.7 Kalubi Clementine
1.1.1.1.8 Tshika + ??
1.1.1.1.8.1 Papy**
1.1.1.1.8.2 Nadege Kakunji
1.1.1.1.8.3 Sandrine Kalonji

1.1.1.1.9 Benjamin Tshiunza

1.1.1.1.10 Mbombo Souzanne + ??
1.1.1.1.10.1 Tshibangu Raphael**
1.1.1.1.10.2 Mukenyi Aimee**

1.1.1.1.11 Mukenyi Aimee + ??
1.1.1.1.11.1 Thethe***
1.1.1.1.11.2 Mukenyi Aimee
1.1.1.1.11.3 Ruphin

1.1.1.2.1 Lukalu Elizabeth + Ntumba Kaboyi
1.1.1.2.1.1 Mitonga Henriette
1.1.1.2.1.2 Ilunga Cele

1.1.1.2.1.3 Mpunga Rosalie
1.1.1.2.1.4 Miandabu
1.1.1.2.1.5 Ting Kasambayi*
1.1.1.2.1.6 Albert Kalonji*
1.1.1.2.1.7 Douglas Kasambayi*
1.1.1.2.1.8 Alain Ilunga***
1.1.1.2.1.9 Chantal
1.1.1.2.1.10 Tshika Marie
1.1.1.2.1.11 Jean Marie

1.1.1.2.2 Sangana + ??
1.1.1.2.2.1 Therese
1.1.1.2.2.2 Kalonji Francois
1.1.1.2.2.3 Mitonga Henriette
1.1.1.2.2.4 Mukuna
1.1.1.2.2.5 Tshibangu Raphael
1.1.1.2.2.6 Tshidibi
1.1.1.2.2.7 Musuamba
1.1.1.2.2.8 Iyowa
1.1.1.2.2.9 Baudoin

1.1.1.2.3 Mukeba Barthelemy + ??
1.1.1.2.3.1 Jean
1.1.1.2.3.2 Mitonga Henriette
1.1.1.2.3.3 Likalu Eliza
1.1.1.2.3.4 Biyuma Buya
1.1.1.2.3.5 Mukeba Sylvie
1.1.1.2.3.6 Sangana

1.1.1.2.4 Masengu

Grands
1.1.1.1.1.1 Tshibangu Raphael***
1.1.1.1.1.1.1 Victor Albert Kalonji***
1.1.1.1.1.1.2 Joyce Kabeya***
1.1.1.1.1.1.3 Raphael Tshibangu***

1.1.1.1.3.1 Noella Kazadi + Paul Sutcha
1.1.1.1.3.1.1 Barbara Sutcha***
1.1.1.1.3.1.2 Jay Sutcha***
1.1.1.1.3.1.3 Rudy***

1.1.1.1.3.2 Joe Mukeba Kazadi****
1.1.1.1.3.2.1 Malaika***

1.1.1.1.3.3 Cocco Mpunga Kazadi + Nana*
1.1.1.1.3.3.1 Moran***
1.1.1.1.3.3.2 Aimee Mukenyi Kazadi*

1.1.1.1.3.5 Felie Kazadi + Eric Kabemba
1.1.1.1.3.5.1 Malikiya Aurore Kabemba

1.1.1.1.3.4 Christine Kamwanya Kazadi Tshibangu + Thomas Muller*****
1.1.1.1.3.4.1 Daniel Mwadianvita Muller*****
1.1.1.1.3.4.2 Elena Mukenyi Muller*****

1.1.1.2.1.1 Mitonga Henriette + ??
1.1.1.2.1.1.1 Diane Biata*
1.1.1.2.1.1.2 Linda Lukalu
1.1.1.2.1.1.3 Lord Ntumba
1.1.1.2.1.1.4 Miandabu
1.1.1.2.1.1.5 Mbuyi
1.1.1.2.1.1.6 Toni
1.1.1.2.1.1.7 Mitonga Henriette
1.1.1.2.1.1.8 Mpunga
1.1.1.2.1.1.9 Olga
1.1.1.2.1.1.10 Carmel
1.1.1.2.1.1.11 Patrick Kambala*

1.1.1.2.1.2 Ilunga Cele + Veronique Misumba Musuala
1.1.1.2.1.2.1 Mpunga Rose*
1.1.1.2.1.2.2 Lukalu Lizette
1.1.1.2.1.2.3 Ntumba Christian
1.1.1.2.1.2.4 Mbuyi Nancy
1.1.1.2.1.2.5 Myriam Mitonga
1.1.1.2.1.2.6 Misumba
1.1.1.2.1.2.7 Mukeba
1.1.1.2.1.2.8 Miandabu Eunice
1.1.1.2.1.2.9 Joe Ntumba*
1.1.1.2.1.2.10 Ruben Kalonji*

1.1.1.2.1.3 Mpunga Rosalie + ??
1.1.1.2.1.3.1 Clarisse
1.1.1.2.1.3.2 Lusamba

1.1.1.2.1.3.3 Ntumba
1.1.1.2.1.3.4 Bambino
1.1.1.2.1.3.5 Kalombo
1.1.1.2.1.3.6 Tshibangu

1.1.1.2.1.5 Ting Kasambayi + Gode*
1.1.1.2.1.5.1 Jerry Kasambayi*
1.1.1.2.1.5.2 Jean-Luc Kasambayi*
1.1.1.2.1.5.3 Deborah Kasambayi*

1.1.1.2.1.6 Albert Kalonji + Michou*
1.1.1.2.1.6.1 Jerry Ntumba*
1.1.1.2.1.6.2 Marc Ntumba*
1.1.1.2.1.6.3 Raphael Tshibangu*

1.1.1.2.1.7 Douglas Kasambayi + Julia*
1.1.1.2.1.7.1 Leeza*
1.1.1.2.1.7.2 Jordan*
1.1.1.2.1.7.3 Jonathan*
1.1.1.2.1.7.4 Leah*

1.1.1.2.1.10 Tshika Marie + ??
1.1.1.2.1.10.1 Mimie*

Great-Grands

1.1.1.2.1.1.1 Diane Biata + Kalonji Joseph*
1.1.1.2.1.1.1.1 Rebecca*
1.1.1.2.1.1.1.1 Curia*
1.1.1.2.1.1.1.1 Linda*
1.1.1.2.1.1.1.1 Clint*

1.1.1.2.1.6.1 Jerry Ntumba + Nicole*
1.1.1.2.1.6.1.1 Skyler*
1.1.1.2.1.6.1.2 Jaze*

1.1.1.2.1.2 Ilunga Cele

1.1.1.2.1.2.1 Mpunga Rose + Gary Campbel*
1.1.1.2.1.2.1.1 Dalyah*
1.1.1.2.1.2.1.2 Darcya*

1.1.1.2.1.10.1 Mimie + Adelar*
1.1.1.2.1.10.1.1 Samuel*
1.1.1.2.1.10.1.2 David*
1.1.1.2.1.10.1.3 Daniel*
1.1.1.2.1.10.1.4 John*

Bibliography

Albert Camus, *The Plague* (1948)

Ngozi Achidie Chimamanga, *That Thing Around Your Neck* (2009)

Roger Daniels, *Coming to America: A History of Immigration and Ethnicity in American Life*, 2nd Edition (2002)

Jared Diamond, *Guns, Germs, and Steel: The Fates of Human Societies* (2017)

Wayne Dyer, *The Power of Intention* (2004); *Change your Thoughts, Change your Life* (2009); *Wishes Fulfilled* (2012)

Frantz Fanon, *The Wretched of The Earth* (1961)

David Gerber, *American Immigration: A Very Short Introduction* (2011)

Adam Hochschild, *King Leopold's Ghost: A Story of Greed, Terror, and Heroism in Colonial Africa* (1999)

Harold Kushner, *When All You've Ever Wanted Isn't Enough* (1986)

Ali A. Mazrui, *The Africans* (1986)

Tshilemalema Mukengo, *Culture and Customs of the Congo* (2001)

Honoré N'Gbanda Nzambo Ko Atumba, *Les Derniers Jours du Maréchal Mobutu* (1998)

Georges Nzongola-Ntalaja, *The Congo from Leopold to Kabila, A People's History* (2002)

Charles Onanga, *Ces Tueurs Tutsi: Au coeur de la tragédie congolaise* (2009)

Linda Barrett Osborne, *This Land Is Our Land: A History of American Immigration* (2016)

John Perkins, *Confessions of an Economic Hit Man* (2004)

Samantha Power, *The Education of An Idealist: A Memoir* (2019)

Joyce Roche, *The Empress Has No Clothes: Conquering Self-Doubt to Embrace Success* (2013)

Malidoma Patrice Some, *The Healing Wisdom of Africa: Finding Purpose Through Nature, Ritual, and Community* (1999)

Jason Stearns, *Dancing in the Glory of Monsters: The Collapse of the Congo and the Great War of Africa (2011)*

Eckhart Tolle, *The Power of Now: A Guide to Spiritual Enlightenment* (1999)

Sanford J. Ungar, *Africa: The People and Politics of an Emerging Continent* (1986)

David Van Reybrouck, *Congo: The Epic History of a People* (2010)

Crawford Young and Thomas Turner, *The Rise and Decline of the Zairean State* (1985)

Raphael T. Tshibangu, M.D.

Acknowledgments

To all who have encouraged and supported me during this endeavor:

To my brother Albert Kalonji, my dear friends and brothers Joe Kazadi and NW Katumba, M.D, for keeping my recollections from straying too far from reality.

To David O'Neil of Story Trust Publishing, for your expertise, professionalism, and patience in editing and designing the book.

And most importantly, to my wife, Sherry, my muse for providing the spark, ongoing support, and encouragement throughout.

I say thank you, with heartfelt appreciation and gratitude.

www.ingramcontent.com/pod-product-compliance
Lightning Source LLC
Chambersburg PA
CBHW040419100526
44589CB00021B/2759